Notes towards
the Definition of Culture

by T. S. Eliot

Notes towards the
DEFINITION
OF CULTURE

T. S. ELIOT

DEFINITION: 1. The setting of bounds;
limitation (rare) – 1483
            —*Oxford English Dictionary*

HARCOURT, BRACE AND COMPANY
NEW YORK

To

PHILIP MAIRET

in gratitude and admiration

Preface

THIS essay was begun four or five years ago. A preliminary sketch, under the same title, was published in three successive numbers of *The New English Weekly*. From this sketch took shape a paper called "Cultural Forces in the Human Order," which appeared in the volume *Prospect for Christendom*, edited by Mr. Maurice B. Reckitt (Faber, 1945): a revision of this paper forms the first chapter of the present book. The second chapter is a revision of a paper published in *The New English Review* in October, 1945.

I have added as an appendix the English text of three broadcast talks to Germany which have appeared under the title of "Die Einheit der Europaeischen Kultur" (Carl Habel Verlagsbuchhandlung, Berlin, 1946).

Throughout this study, I recognise a particular debt to the writings of Canon V. A. Demant, Mr. Christopher Dawson, and the late Professor Karl Mannheim. It is the more necessary to acknowledge this debt in general, since I have not in my text referred to the first two of these writers, and since my debt to the third is much greater than appears from the one context in which I discuss his theory.

I have also profited by reading an article by Mr. Dwight Macdonald in *Politics* (New York) for February 1944, entitled "A Theory of 'Popular Culture'"; and an anonymous critique of this article in the issue of the same periodical for November 1946. Mr. Macdonald's theory strikes me as the best *alternative* to my own that I have seen.

T. S. E.

January, 1948.

Contents

Introduction

I think our studies ought to be all but purposeless. They want to be pursued with chastity like mathematics.—ACTON.

MY purpose in writing the following chapters is not, as might appear from a casual inspection of the table of contents, to outline a social or political philosophy; nor is the book intended to be merely a vehicle for my observations on a variety of topics. My aim is to help to define a word, the word *culture*.

Just as a doctrine only needs to be defined after the appearance of some heresy, so a word does not need to receive this attention until it has come to be misused. I have observed with growing anxiety the career of this word *culture* during the past six or seven years. We may find it natural, and significant, that during a period of unparalleled destructiveness, this word should come to have an important role in the journalistic vocabulary. Its part is of course doubled by the word *civilisation*. I have made no attempt in this essay to determine the frontier between the meanings of these two words: for I came to the conclusion that any such attempt could only produce an artificial distinction, peculiar to the book, which the reader would have difficulty in retaining; and which, after closing the book, he would abandon with a sense of relief. We do use one word, frequently enough, in a context where the other would do as well; there are other contexts where one word obviously fits and the other does not; and I do not think that this need cause embarrassment. There are enough inevitable obstacles, in this discussion, without erecting unnecessary ones.

In August, 1945, there was published the text of a draft constitution for a "United Nations Educational Scientific and Cultural Organisation." The purpose of this organisation was, in Article I, defined as follows:

1. To develop and maintain mutual understanding and appreciation of the life and culture, the arts, the humanities, and the sciences of the peoples of the world, as a basis for effective international organisation and world peace.

2. To co-operate in extending and in making available to all peoples for the service of common human needs the world's full body of knowledge and culture, and in assuring its contribution to the economic stability, political security, and general well-being of the peoples of the world.

I am not at the moment concerned to extract a meaning from these sentences: I only quote them to call attention to the word *culture,* and to suggest that before acting on such resolutions we should try to find out what this one word means. This is only one of innumerable instances which might be cited, of the use of a word which nobody bothers to examine. In general, the word is used in two ways: by a kind of synecdoche, when the speaker has in mind one of the elements or evidences of culture—such as "art"; or, as in the passage just quoted, as a kind of emotional stimulant—or anaesthetic.[1]

[1] The use of the word *culture,* by those who have not, as it seems to me, pondered deeply on the meaning of the word before employing it, might be illustrated by countless examples. Another instance may suffice. I quote from the *Times Educational Supplement* of November 3, 1945 (p. 522):

" 'Why should we bring into our scheme for international collaboration machinery concerning education and culture?' Such was the question asked by the Prime Minister when, in addressing the delegates of nearly 40 nations attending the United Nations Conference to establish an Educational and Cultural Organisation in London on Thursday afternoon, he extended to them the greetings of His Majesty's Government. . . . Mr. Attlee concluded with a plea that if we were to know our neighbours we must understand their culture, through their books, newspapers, radio and films."

The Minister of Education committed herself to the following:

"Now we are met together: workers in education, in scientific re-

Introduction

At the beginning of my first chapter I have endeavoured to distinguish and relate the three principal uses of the word: and to make the point, that when we use the term in one of these three ways we should do so in awareness of the others. I then try to expose the essential relation of culture to religion, and to make clear the limitations of the word *relation* as an expression of this "relation." The first important assertion is that no culture has appeared or developed except together with a religion: according to the point of view of the observer, the culture will appear to be the product of the religion, or the religion the product of the culture.

In the next three chapters I discuss what seem to me to be three important conditions for culture. The first of these is organic (not merely planned, but growing) structure, such as will foster the hereditary transmission of culture within a culture: and this requires the persistence of social classes. The second is the necessity that a culture should be analysable, geographically, into local cultures: this raises the problem of "regionalism." The third is the balance of unity and diversity in religion—that is, universality of doctrine with particularity

search, and in the varied fields of culture. We represent those who teach, those who discover, those who write, those who express their inspiration in music or in art. . . . Lastly we have culture. Some may argue that the artist, the musician, the writer, all the creative workers in the humanities and the arts, cannot be organised either nationally or internationally. The artist, it has been said, works to please himself. That might have been a tenable argument before the war. But those of us who remember the struggle in the Far East and in Europe in the days preceding the open war know how much the fight against Fascism depended upon the determination of writers and artists to keep their international contacts that they might reach across the rapidly rising frontier barriers."

It is only fair to add, that when it comes to talking nonsense about culture, there is nothing to choose between politicians of one stripe or another. Had the election of 1945 brought the alternative party into power, we should have heard much the same pronouncements in the same circumstances. The pursuit of politics is incompatible with a strict attention to exact meanings on all occasions. The reader should therefore abstain from deriding either Mr. Attlee or the late regretted Miss Wilkinson.

of cult and devotion. The reader must keep in mind that I am not pretending to account for all the necessary conditions for a flourishing culture; I discuss three which have especially struck my attention.[1] He must also remember that what I offer is not a set of directions for fabricating a culture. I do not say that by setting about to produce these, and any other additional conditions, we can confidently expect to improve our civilisation. I say only that, so far as my observation goes, you are unlikely to have a high civilisation where these conditions are absent.

The remaining two chapters of the book make some slight attempt to disentangle culture from politics and education.

I dare say that some readers will draw political inferences from this discussion: what is more likely is that particular minds will read into my text a confirmation or repudiation of their own political convictions and prejudices. The writer himself is not without political convictions and prejudices; but the imposition of them is no part of his present intention. What I try to say is this: here are what I believe to be essential conditions for the growth and for the survival of culture. If they conflict with any passionate faith of the reader —if, for instance, he finds it shocking that culture and equalitarianism should conflict, if it seems monstrous to him that anyone should have "advantages of birth"—I do not ask him

[1] In an illuminating supplement to the *Christian News-Letter* of July 24, 1946, Miss Marjorie Reeves has a very suggestive paragraph on "The Culture of an Industry." If she somewhat enlarged her meaning, what she says would fit in with my own way of using the word "culture." She says, of the culture of an industry, which she believes quite rightly should be presented to the young worker: "it includes the geography of its raw materials and final markets, its historical evolution, inventions and scientific background, its economics and so forth." It includes all this, certainly; but an industry, if it is to engage the interest of more than the conscious mind of the worker, should also have a way of life somewhat peculiar to its initiates, with its own forms of festivity and observances. I mention this interesting reminder of the culture of industry, however, as evidence that I am aware of other nuclei of culture than those discussed in this book.

tion that we can ask, is whether there is any permanent standard, by which we can compare one civilisation with another, and by which we can make some guess at the improvement or decline of our own. We have to admit, in comparing one civilisation with another, and in comparing the different stages of our own, that no one society and no one age of it realises all the values of civilisation. Not all of these values may be compatible with each other: what is at least as certain is that in realising some we lose the appreciation of others. Nevertheless, we can distinguish between higher and lower cultures; we can distinguish between advance and retrogression. We can assert with some confidence that our own period is one of decline; that the standards of culture are lower than they were fifty years ago; and that the evidences of this decline are visible in every department of human activity.[1] I see no reason why the decay of culture should not proceed much further, and why we may not even anticipate a period, of some duration, of which it is possible to say that it will have *no* culture. Then culture will have to grow again from the soil; and when I say it must grow again from the soil, I do not mean that it will be brought into existence by any activity of political demagogues. The question asked by this essay, is whether there are any permanent conditions, in the absence of which no higher culture can be expected.

If we succeed even partially in answering this question, we must then put ourselves on guard against the delusion of trying to bring about these conditions *for the sake of* the improvement of our culture. For if any definite conclusions emerge from this study, one of them is surely this, that culture is the one thing that we cannot deliberately aim at. It is the product of a variety of more or less harmonious activities, each pursued for its own sake: the artist must concentrate

---

[1] For confirmation from a point of view very different from that from which this essay is written, see *Our Threatened Values* by Victor Gollancz (1946).

upon his canvas, the poet upon his typewriter, the civil servant upon the just settlement of particular problems as they present themselves upon his desk, each according to the situation in which he finds himself. Even if these conditions with which I am concerned, seem to the reader to represent desirable social aims, he must not leap to the conclusion that these aims can be fulfilled solely by deliberate organisation. A class division of society planned by an absolute authority would be artificial and intolerable; a decentralisation under central direction would be a contradiction; an ecclesiastical unity cannot be imposed in the hope that it will bring about unity of faith, and a religious diversity cultivated for its own sake would be absurd. The point at which we can arrive, is the recognition that these conditions of culture are "natural" to human beings; that although we can do little to encourage them, we can combat the intellectual errors and the emotional prejudices which stand in their way. For the rest, we should look for the improvement of society, as we seek our own individual improvement, in relatively minute particulars. We cannot say: "I shall make myself into a different person"; we can only say: "I will give up this bad habit, and endeavour to contract this good one." So of society we can only say: "We shall try to improve it in this respect or the other, where excess or defect is evident; we must try at the same time to embrace so much in our view, that we may avoid, in putting one thing right, putting something else wrong." Even this is to express an aspiration greater than we can achieve: for it is as much, or more, because of what we do piecemeal without understanding or foreseeing the consequences, that the culture of one age differs from that of its predecessor.

CHAPTER I

The Three Senses of "Culture"

THE term *culture* has different associations according to whether we have in mind the development of an *individual,* of a *group* or *class,* or of a *whole society.* It is a part of my thesis that the culture of the individual is dependent upon the culture of a group or class, and that the culture of the group or class is dependent upon the culture of the whole society to which that group or class belongs. Therefore it is the culture of the society that is fundamental, and it is the meaning of the term "culture" in relation to the whole society that should be examined first. When the term "culture" is applied to the manipulation of lower organisms —to the work of the bacteriologist or the *agri*culturalist— the meaning is clear enough, for we can have unanimity in respect of the ends to be attained, and we can agree when we have or have not attained them. When it is applied to the improvement of the human mind and spirit, we are less likely to agree as to what culture is. The term itself, as signifying something to be consciously aimed at in human affairs, has not a long history. As something to be achieved by deliberate effort, "culture" is relatively intelligible when we are concerned with the self-cultivation of the individual, whose culture is seen against the background of the culture of the group and of the society. The culture of the group also has a definite meaning in contrast to the less developed culture of the mass of society. The difference between the three applications of the term can be best apprehended by asking how far, in relation to the individual, the group, and society as a whole the *conscious aim to achieve culture* has any meaning. A good deal of confusion could be avoided, if we refrained from setting before the group, what can be the aim only of the individual; and before society as a whole, what can be the aim only of a group.

The general, or anthropological sense of the word *culture,* as used for instance by E. B. Tylor in the title of his book *Primitive Culture,* has flourished independently of the other senses: but if we are considering highly developed societies, and especially our own contemporary society, we have to consider the relationship of the three senses. At this point anthropology passes over into sociology. Amongst men of letters and moralists, it has been usual to discuss culture in the first two senses, and especially the first, without relation to the third. The most easily remembered example of this selection is Matthew Arnold's *Culture and Anarchy.* Arnold is concerned primarily with the individual and the "perfection" at which he should aim. It is true that in his famous classification of "Barbarians, Philistines, Populace" he concerns himself with a critique of classes; but his criticism is confined to an indictment of these classes for their shortcomings, and does not proceed to consider what should be the proper function or "perfection" of each class. The effect, therefore, is to exhort the individual who would attain the peculiar kind of "perfection" which Arnold calls "culture," to rise superior to the limitations of any class, rather than to realise its highest attainable ideals.

The impression of thinness which Arnold's "culture" conveys to a modern reader is partly due to the absence of social background to his picture. But it is also due, I think, to his failure to take account of another way in which we use the word "culture," besides the three already mentioned. There are several kinds of attainment which we may have in mind in different contexts. We may be thinking of refinement of manners—or *urbanity* and *civility:* if so, we shall think first of a social class, and of the superior individual as representative of the best of that class. We may be thinking of *learning* and a close acquaintance with the accumulated wisdom of the past: if so, our man of culture is the scholar. We may be thinking of *philosophy* in the widest sense—an interest in, and some ability to manipulate, abstract ideas: if so, we may mean the intellectual (recognising the fact that this term is now used very loosely, to comprehend many persons not conspicuous for strength of intellect). Or we may be thinking of *the arts:* if so, we mean the artist and the amateur or dilettante. But what we seldom have in mind is all of these things at the same time. We do not find, for instance, that an understanding of music or painting figures explicitly in Arnold's description of the cultured man: yet no one will deny that these attainments play a part in culture.

If we look at the several activities of culture listed in the preceding paragraph, we must conclude that no perfection in any one of them, to the exclusion of the others, can confer culture on anybody. We know that good manners, without education, intellect or sensibility to the arts, tends towards mere automatism; that learning without good manners or sensibility is pedantry; that intellectual ability without the more human attributes is admirable only in the same way as the brilliance of a child chess prodigy; and that the arts without intellectual context are vanity. And if we do not find culture in any one of these perfections alone, so we must not expect any one person to be accomplished in all of them; we shall come to infer that the wholly cultured individual is a phantasm; and we shall look for culture, not in any individual or in any one group of individuals, but more and more widely; and we are driven in the end to find it in the pattern of the society as a whole. This seems to me a very obvious reflection: but it is frequently overlooked. People are always ready to consider themselves persons of culture, on the strength of one proficiency, when they are not only lacking in others, but blind to those they lack. An artist of any kind, even a very great artist, is not for this reason alone a man of culture: artists are not only often insensitive to other arts than those which they practise, but sometimes have very bad manners or meagre intellectual gifts. The person who contributes to culture, however important his contribution may be, is not always a "cultured person."

It does not follow from this that there is no meaning in speaking of the culture of an individual, or of a group or class. We only mean that the culture of the individual cannot be isolated from that of the group, and that the culture of the group cannot be abstracted from that of the whole society; and that our notion of "perfection" must take all three senses of "culture" into account at once. Nor does it follow that in a society, of whatever grade of culture, the groups concerned with each activity of culture will be distinct and exclusive: on the contrary, it is only by an overlapping and sharing of interests, by participation and mutual appreciation, that the cohesion necessary for culture can obtain. A religion requires not only a body of priests who know what they are doing, but a body of worshippers who know what is being done.

It is obvious that among the more primitive communities the several activities of culture are inextricably interwoven. The Dyak who spends the better part of a season in shaping, carving and painting his barque of the peculiar design required for the annual ritual of head-hunting, is exercising several cultural activities at once—of art and religion, as well as of amphibious warfare. As civilisation becomes more complex, greater occupational specialisation evinces itself: in the "stone age" New Hebrides, Mr. John Layard says, certain islands specialise in particular arts and crafts, exchanging their wares and displaying their accomplishments to the reciprocal satisfaction of the members of the archipelago. But while the individuals of a tribe, or of a group of islands or villages, may have separate functions—of which the most peculiar are those of the king and the witch-doctor—it is only at a much further stage that religion, science, politics and art become abstractly conceived apart from each other. And just as the functions of individuals become hereditary, and hereditary function hardens into class or caste distinction, and class distinction leads to conflict, so do religion, politics, science and art reach a point at which there is conscious struggle between them for autonomy or dominance. This friction is, at some stages and in some situations, highly creative: how far it is the result, and how far the cause, of increased consciousness need not here be considered. The tension within the society may become also a tension within the mind of the more conscious individual: the clash of duties in *Antigone,* which is not simply a clash between piety and civil obedience, or between religion and politics, but between conflicting laws within what is still a religious-political complex, represents a very advanced stage of civilisation: for the conflict must have meaning in the audience's experience before it can be made articulate by the dramatist and receive from the audience the response which the dramatist's art requires.

As a society develops towards functional complexity and differentiation, we may expect the emergence of several cultural levels: in short, the culture of the class or group will present itself. It will not, I think, be disputed that in any future society, as in every civilised society of the past, there must be these different levels. I do not think that the most ardent champions of social equality dispute this: the difference of opinion turns on whether the transmission of group culture must be by inheritance—whether each cultural level must propagate itself—or whether it can be hoped that some mechanism of selection will be found, so that every individual

shall in due course take his place at the highest cultural level
for which his natural aptitudes qualify him. What is pertinent at this point is that the emergence of more highly cultured groups does not leave the rest of society unaffected: it
is itself part of a process in which the whole society changes.
And it is certain—and especially obvious when we turn our
attention to the arts—that as new values appear, and as
thought, sensibility and expression become more elaborate,
some earlier values vanish. That is only to say that you cannot expect to have all stages of development at once; that a
civilisation cannot simultaneously produce great folk poetry
at one cultural level and *Paradise Lost* at another. Indeed,
the one thing that time is ever sure to bring about is the loss:
gain or compensation is almost always conceivable but never
certain.

While it appears that progress in civilisation will bring
into being more specialised culture groups, we must not
expect this development to be unattended by perils. Cultural
disintegration may ensue upon cultural specialisation: and
it is the most radical disintegration that a society can suffer.
It is not the only kind, or it is not the only aspect, under
which disintegration can be studied; but, whatever be cause
or effect, the disintegration of culture is the most serious and
the most difficult to repair. (Here, of course, we are empha-
sising the culture of the whole society.) It must not be confused with another malady, ossification into caste, as in Hindu
India, of what may have been originally only a hierarchy of
functions: even though it is possible that both maladies have
some hold upon British society today. Cultural disintegration
is present when two or more strata so separate that these
become in effect distinct cultures; and also when culture at
the upper group level breaks into fragments each of which
represents one cultural activity alone. If I am not mistaken,
some disintegration of the classes in which culture is, or
should be, most highly developed, has already taken place in
western society—as well as some cultural separation between

one level of society and another. Religious thought and practice, philosophy and art, all tend to become isolated areas cultivated by groups in no communication with each other. The artistic sensibility is impoverished by its divorce from the religious sensibility, the religious by its separation from the artistic; and the vestige of *manners* may be left to a few survivors of a vanishing class who, their sensibility untrained by either religion or art and their minds unfurnished with the material for witty conversation, will have no context in their lives to give value to their behaviour. And deterioration on the higher levels is a matter of concern, not only to the group which is visibly affected, but to the whole people.

The causes of a total decline of culture are as complex as the evidence of it is various. Some may be found in the accounts given, by various specialists, of the causes of more readily apprehended social ailments for which we must continue to seek specific remedies. Yet we become more and more aware of the extent to which the baffling problem of "culture" underlies the problems of the relation of every part of the world to every other. When we concern ourselves with the relation of the great nations to each other; the relation of the great to the small nations;[1] the relation of intermixed "communities," as in India, to each other; the relation of parent nations to those which have originated as colonies; the relation of the colonist to the native; the relation between peoples of such areas as the West Indies, where compulsion or economic inducement has brought together large

[1] This point is touched upon, though without any discussion of the meaning of "culture," by E. H. Carr: *Conditions of Peace,* Part I, ch. iii. He says: "In a clumsy but convenient terminology which originated in Central Europe, we must distinguish between 'cultural nation' and 'state nation.' The existence of a more or less homogeneous racial or linguistic group bound together by a common tradition and the cultivation of a common culture must cease to provide a *prima facie* case for the setting up or the maintenance of an independent political unit." But Mr. Carr is here concerned with the problem of political unity, rather than with that of the preservation of cultures, or the question whether they are worth preserving, in the political unit.

25

numbers of different races: behind all these perplexing questions, involving decisions to be made by many men every day, there is the question of what culture is, and the question whether it is anything that we can control or deliberately influence. These questions confront us whenever we devise a theory, or frame a policy, of education. If we take culture seriously, we see that a people does not need merely enough to eat (though even that is more than we seem able to ensure) but a proper and particular *cuisine:* one symptom of the decline of culture in Britain is indifference to the art of preparing food. Culture may even be described simply as that which makes life worth living. And it is what justifies other peoples and other generations in saying, when they contemplate the remains and the influence of an extinct civilisation, that it was *worth while* for that civilisation to have existed.

I have already asserted, in my introduction, that no culture can appear or develop except in relation to a religion. But the use of the term *relation* here may easily lead us into error. The facile assumption of a relationship between culture and religion is perhaps the most fundamental weakness of Arnold's *Culture and Anarchy.* Arnold gives the impression that Culture (as he uses the term) is something more comprehensive than religion; that the latter is no more than a necessary element, supplying ethical formation and some emotional colour, to Culture which is the ultimate value.

It may have struck the reader that what I have said about the development of culture, and about the dangers of disintegration when a culture has reached a highly developed stage, may apply also in the history of religion. The development of culture and the development of religion, in a society uninfluenced from without, cannot be clearly isolated from each other: and it will depend upon the bias of the particular observer, whether a refinement of culture is held to be the cause of progress in religion, or whether a progress in religion is held to be the cause of a refinement of the culture. What perhaps influences us towards treating religion and culture as two different things is the history of the penetration of Graeco-Roman culture by the Christian Faith—a penetration which had profound effects both upon that culture and upon the course of development taken by Christian thought and practice. But the culture with which primitive Christianity came into contact (as well as that of the environment in which Christianity took its origins) was itself a religious culture in decline. So, while we believe that the same religion may inform a variety of cultures, we may ask whether any culture could come into being, or maintain itself, without a religious basis. We may go further and ask whether what we call the culture, and what we call the religion, of a people are not different aspects of the same thing: the culture being, essentially, the incarnation (so to speak) of the religion of a people. To put the matter in this way may throw light on my reservations concerning the word *relation*.

As a society develops, a greater number of degrees and kinds of religious capacity and function—as well as of other capacities and functions—will make their appearance. It is to be noticed that in some religions the differentiation has been so wide that there have resulted in effect two religions—one for the populace and one for the adepts. The evils of "two nations" in religion are obvious. Christianity has resisted this malady better than Hinduism. The schisms of the sixteenth century, and the subsequent multiplication of sects, can be studied either as the history of division of religious thought, or as a struggle between opposing social groups—as the variation of doctrine, or as the disintegration of European culture. Yet, while these wide divergences of belief on the same level are lamentable, the Faith can, and must, find room for many degrees of intellectual, imaginative and emotional receptivity to the same doctrines, just as it can embrace many variations of order and ritual. The Christian Faith also, psychologically considered—as systems of beliefs and attitudes in particular embodied minds—will have a history: though it would be a gross error to suppose that the sense in which it can be spoken of as developing and changing, implies the possibility of greater sanctity or divine illumination becoming available to human beings through collective progress. (We do not assume that there is, over a long period, progress even in art, or that "primitive" art is, as art, necessarily inferior to the more sophisticated.) But one of the features of development, whether we are taking the religious or the cultural point of view, is the appearance of *scepticism*—by which, of course, I do not mean infidelity or destructiveness (still less the unbelief which is due to mental sloth) but the habit of examining evidence and the capacity for delayed decision. Scepticism is a highly civilised trait, though, when it declines into pyrrhonism, it is one of which civilisation can die. Where scepticism is strength, pyrrhonism is weakness: for we need not only the strength to defer a decision, but the strength to make one.

The conception of culture and religion as being, when each term is taken in the right context, different aspects of the same thing, is one which requires a good deal of explanation. But I should like to suggest first, that it provides us with the means of combating two complementary errors. The one more widely held is that culture can be preserved, extended and developed in the absence of religion. This error may be held by the Christian in common with the infidel, and its proper refutation would require an historical analysis of considerable refinement, because the truth is not immediately apparent, and may seem even to be contradicted by appearances: a culture may linger on, and indeed produce some of its most brilliant artistic and other successes after the religious faith has fallen into decay. The other error is the belief that the preservation and maintenance of religion need not reckon with the preservation and maintenance of culture: a belief which may even lead to the rejection of the products of culture as frivolous obstructions to the spiritual life. To be in a position to reject this error, as with the other, requires us to take a distant view; to refuse to accept the conclusion, when the culture that we see is a culture in decline, that culture is something to which we can afford to remain indifferent. And I must add that to see the unity of culture and religion in this way neither implies that all the products of art can be accepted uncritically, nor provides a criterion by which everybody can immediately distinguish between them. Esthetic sensibility must be extended into spiritual perception, and spiritual perception must be extended into esthetic sensibility and disciplined taste before we are qualified to pass judgment upon decadence or diabolism or nihilism in art. To judge a work of art by artistic or by religious standards, to judge a religion by religious or artistic standards should come in the end to the same thing: though it is an end at which no individual can arrive.

The way of looking at culture and religion which I have been trying to adumbrate is so difficult that I am not sure I grasp it myself except in flashes, or that I comprehend all its implications. It is also one which involves the risk of error at every moment, by some unperceived alteration of the meaning which either term has when the two are coupled in this way, into some meaning which either may have when taken alone. It holds good only in the sense in which people are unconscious of both their culture and their religion. Anyone with even the slightest religious consciousness must be afflicted from time to time by the contrast between his religious faith and his behaviour; anyone with the taste that *individual* or *group* culture confers must be aware of values which he cannot call religious. And both "religion" and "culture," besides meaning different things from each other, should mean for the individual and for the group something towards which they strive, not merely something which they possess. Yet there is an aspect in which we can see a religion as the *whole way of life* of a people, from birth to the grave, from morning to night and even in sleep, and that way of life is also its culture. And at the same time we must recognise that when this identification is complete, it means in actual societies both an inferior culture and an inferior religion. A universal religion is at least potentially higher than one which any race or nation claims exclusively for itself; and a culture realising a religion also realised in other cultures is at least potentially a higher culture than one which has a religion exclusively to itself. From one point of view we may identify: from another, we must separate.

Taking now the point of view of identification, the reader must remind himself, as the author has constantly to do, of how much is here embraced by the term *culture*. It includes all the characteristic activities and interests of a people: Derby Day, Henley Regatta, Cowes, the twelfth of August, a cup final, the dog races, the pin table, the dart board, Wensleydale cheese, boiled cabbage cut into sections, beetroot in vinegar, nineteenth-century Gothic churches and the music of Elgar. The reader can make his own list. And then we have to face the strange idea that what is part of our culture is also a part of our *lived* religion.

We must not think of our culture as completely unified— my list above was designed to avoid that suggestion. And the actual religion of no European people has ever been purely Christian, or purely anything else. There are always bits and traces of more primitive faiths, more or less absorbed; there is always the tendency towards parasitic beliefs; there are always perversions, as when patriotism, which pertains to natural religion and is therefore licit and even encouraged by the Church, becomes exaggerated into a caricature of itself. And it is only too easy for a people to maintain contradictory beliefs and to propitiate mutually antagonistic powers.

The reflection that what we believe is not merely what we formulate and subscribe to, but that behaviour is also belief, and that even the most conscious and developed of us live also at the level on which belief and behaviour cannot be distinguished, is one that may, once we allow our imagination to play upon it, be very disconcerting. It gives an importance to our most trivial pursuits, to the occupation of our every minute, which we cannot contemplate long without the horror of nightmare. When we consider the quality of the integration required for the full cultivation of the spiritual life, we must keep in mind the possibility of grace and the exemplars of sanctity in order not to sink into despair. And when we consider the problem of evangelisation, of the development of a Christian society, we have reason to quail. To believe that *we* are religious people and that other people are without religion is a simplification which approaches distortion. To reflect that from one point of view religion is culture, and from another point of view culture is religion, can be very disturbing. To ask whether the people have not a religion already, in which Derby Day and the dog track play their parts, is embarrassing; so is the suggestion that part of the religion of the higher ecclesiastic is gaiters and the Athenaeum. It is inconvenient for Christians to find that as Christians they do not believe enough, and that on the other hand they, with everybody else, believe in too many things: yet this is a consequence of reflecting, that bishops are a part of English culture, and horses and dogs are a part of English religion.

It is commonly assumed that there is culture, but that it is the property of a small section of society; and from this assumption it is usual to proceed to one of two conclusions: either that culture can only be the concern of a small minority, and that therefore there is no place for it in the society of the future; or that in the society of the future the culture which has been the possession of the few must be put at the disposal of everybody. This assumption and its consequences remind us of the Puritan antipathy to monasticism and the ascetic life: for just as a culture which is only accessible to the few is now deprecated, so was the enclosed and contemplative life condemned by extreme Protestantism, and celibacy regarded with almost as much abhorrence as perversion.

In order to apprehend the theory of religion and culture which I have endeavoured to set forth in this chapter, we have to try to avoid the two alternative errors: that of regarding religion and culture as two separate things between which there is a *relation,* and that of *identifying* religion and culture. I spoke at one point of the culture of a people as an *incarnation* of its religion; and while I am aware of the temerity of employing such an exalted term, I cannot think of any other which would convey so well the intention to avoid *relation* on the one hand and *identification* on the other. The truth, partial truth, or falsity of a religion neither consists in the cultural achievements of the peoples professing that religion, nor submits to being exactly tested by them. For what a people may be said to believe, as shown by its behaviour, is, as I have said, always a great deal more and a great deal less than its professed faith in its purity. Furthermore, a people whose culture has been formed together with a religion of partial truth, may live that religion (at some period in its history, at least) with greater fidelity than another people which has a truer light. It is only when we imagine our culture as it ought to be, if our society were a really Christian society, that we can dare to speak of Christian culture as the highest culture; it is only by referring to all the phases of this culture, which has been the culture of Europe, that we can affirm that it is the highest culture that the world has ever known. In comparing our culture as it is today, with that of non-Christian peoples, we must be prepared to find that ours is in one respect or another inferior. I do not overlook the possibility that Britain, if it consummated its apostasy by reforming itself according to the prescriptions of some inferior or materialistic religion, might blossom into a culture more brilliant than that we can show today. That would not be evidence that the new religion was true, and that Christianity was false. It would merely prove that any religion, while it lasts, and on its own level, gives an apparent meaning to life, provides the framework for a culture, and protects the mass of humanity from boredom and despair.

CHAPTER II

The Class and the Elite

IT would appear, according to the account of levels of culture put forward in the previous chapter, that among the more primitive societies, the higher types exhibit more marked differentiations of function amongst their members than the lower types.[1] At a higher stage still, we find that some functions are more honoured than others, and this division promotes the development of *classes*, in which higher honour and higher privilege are accorded, not merely to the person as functionary but as member of the class. And the class itself possesses a function, that of maintaining that part of the total culture of the society which pertains to that class. We have to try to keep in mind, that in a healthy society this maintenance of a particular level of culture is to the benefit, not merely of the class which maintains it, but of the society as a whole. Awareness of this fact will prevent us from supposing that the culture of a "higher" class is something superfluous to society as a whole, or to the majority, and from supposing that it is something which ought to be shared equally by all other classes. It should also remind the "higher"

[1] I am anxious to avoid speaking as if the evolution of primitive culture to higher forms was a process which we knew by observation. We *observe* the differences, we *infer* that some have developed from a stage similar to that of the lower stages which we observe: but however legitimate our inference, I am here not concerned with that development.

class, in so far as any such exists, that the survival of the culture in which it is particularly interested is dependent upon the health of the culture of the people.

It has now become a commonplace of contemporary thinking, that a society thus articulated is not the highest type to which we may aspire; but that it is indeed in the nature of things for a progressive society eventually to overcome these divisions, and that it is also within the power of our conscious direction, and therefore a duty incumbent upon us, to bring about a classless society. But while it is generally supposed that class, in any sense which maintains associations of the past, will disappear, it is now the opinion of some of the most advanced minds that some qualitative differences between individuals must still be recognised, and that the superior individuals must be formed into suitable groups, endowed with appropriate powers, and perhaps with varied emoluments and honours. Those groups, formed of individuals apt for powers of government and administration, will direct the public life of the nation; the individuals composing them will be spoken of as "leaders." There will be groups concerned with art, and groups concerned with science, and groups concerned with philosophy, as well as groups consisting of men of action: and these groups are what we call élites.

It is obvious, that while in the present state of society there is found the voluntary association of like-minded individuals, and association based upon common material interest, or common occupation or profession, the élites of the future will differ in one important respect from any that we know: they will replace the classes of the past, whose positive functions they will assume. This transformation is not always explicitly stated. There are some philosophers who regard class divisions as intolerable, and others who regard them merely as moribund. The latter may simply ignore class, in their design for an élite-governed society, and say that the élites will "be drawn from all sections of society." But it would seem that as we perfect the means for identifying at an early age, educating for their future role, and settling into positions of authority, the individuals who will form the élites, all former class distinctions will become a mere shadow or vestige, and the only social distinction of rank will be between the élites and the rest of the community, unless, as may happen, there is to be an order of precedence and prestige amongst the several élites themselves.

However moderately and unobtrusively the doctrine of élites is put, it implies a radical transformation of society. Superficially, it appears to aim at no more than what we must all desire—that all positions in society should be occupied by those who are best fitted to exercise the functions of the positions. We have all observed individuals occupying situations in life for which neither their character nor their intellect qualified them, and so placed only through nominal education, or birth or consanguinity. No honest man but is vexed by such a spectacle. But the doctrine of élites implies a good deal more than the rectification of such injustice. It posits an *atomic* view of society.

The philosopher whose views on the subject of élites deserve the closest attention, both for their own value and because of the influence they exert, is the late Dr. Karl Mannheim. It is, for that matter, Dr. Mannheim who has founded the fortunes, in this country, of the term élite. I must remark that Dr. Mannheim's description of culture is different from that given in the previous chapter of this essay. He says:

A sociological investigation of culture in liberal society must begin with the life of those who create culture, i.e. the intelligentsia and their position within society as a whole.[1]

According to the account which I have given, a "culture" is conceived as the creation of the society as a whole: being, from another aspect, that which makes it a society. It is not

[1] P. 81, *Man and Society in an Age of Reconstruction,* 1940, New York, Harcourt, Brace.

the creation of any one part of that society. The function of what Dr. Mannheim would call the culture-creating groups, according to my account, would be rather to bring about a further development of the culture in organic complexity: culture at a more conscious level, but still the same culture. This higher level of culture must be thought of both as valuable in itself, and as enriching the lower levels: thus the movement of culture would proceed in a kind of cycle, each class nourishing the others.

This is, already, a difference of some importance. My next observation is that Dr. Mannheim is concerned rather with élites than with an élite.

We may distinguish [he says, in *Man and Society*, p. 82] the following types of élites: the political, the organising, the intellectual, the artistic, the moral and the religious. Whereas the political and organising élites aim at integrating a great number of individual wills, it is the function of the intellectual, aesthetic, and moral-religious élites to sublimate those psychic energies which society, in the daily struggle for existence, does not fully exhaust.

This departmentalisation of élites already exists, to some extent; and to some extent it is a necessary and a good thing. But, so far as it can be observed to exist, it is not *altogether* a good thing. I have suggested elsewhere that a growing weakness of our culture has been the increasing isolation of élites from each other, so that the political, the philosophical, the artistic, the scientific, are separated to the great loss of each of them, not merely through the arrest of any general circulation of ideas, but through the lack of those contacts and mutual influences at a less conscious level, which are perhaps even more important than ideas. The problem of the formation, preservation and development of the élites is therefore also the problem of the formation, preservation and development of *the* élite, a problem upon which Dr. Mannheim does not touch.

As an introduction to this problem, I must draw attention

to another difference between my view and that of Dr. Mannheim. He observes, in a passage which I think contains an
important truth (p. 85):

The crisis of culture in liberal-democratic society is due, in the
first place, to the fact that the fundamental social processes, which
previously favoured the development of the culturally creative élites,
now have the opposite effect, i.e. have become obstacles to the forming
of élites because wider sections of the population take an active part
in cultural activities.

I cannot, of course, admit the last clause of this sentence as
it stands. According to my view of culture, the whole of the
population *should* "take an active part in cultural activities"
—not all in the same activities or on the same level. What this
clause means, in my terms, is that an increasing proportion
of the population is concerned with group culture. This
comes about, I think Dr. Mannheim would agree, through
the gradual alteration of the class-structure. But at this point
it seems to me that Dr. Mannheim begins to confuse élite
with *class*. For he says (p. 89):

If one calls to mind the essential forms of selecting élites which up
to the present have appeared on the historical scene, three principles
can be distinguished: selection on the basis of *blood, property* and
achievement. Aristocratic society, especially after it had entrenched
itself, chose its élites primarily on the blood principle. Bourgeois
society gradually introduced, as a supplement, the principle of
wealth, a principle which also obtained for the intellectual élite,
inasmuch as education was more or less available only to the offspring of the well-to-do. It is, of course, true that the principle of
achievement was combined with the two other principles in earlier
periods, but it is the important contribution of modern democracy
as long as it is rigorous, that the achievement principle increasingly
tends to become the criterion of social success.

I am ready to accept, in a rough and ready way, this account
of three historical periods. But I would remark that we are
here not concerned with élites but with *classes* or, more precisely, with the evolution from a class to a classless society.

It seems to me that at the stage of the sharpest division into classes we can distinguish an élite also. Are we to believe that the artists of the Middle Ages were all men of noble rank, or that the hierarchy and the statesmen were all selected according to their pedigrees?

I do not think that this is what Dr. Mannheim wishes us to believe; but I think that he is confusing the élites with the dominant section of society which the élites served, from which they took their colour, and into which some of their individual members were recruited. The general scheme of the transition of society, in the last five hundred years or so, is usually accepted, and I have no interest in questioning it. I would only propose one qualification. At the stage of dominance of *bourgeois* society (I think it would be more exact to say here, "upper middle class society") there is a difference applying particularly to England. However powerful it was—for its power is now commonly said to be passing—it would not have been what it was, without the existence of a class above it, from which it drew some of its ideals and some of its criteria, and to the condition of which its more ambitious members aspired. This gives it a difference in kind from the aristocratic society which preceded it, and from the mass-society which is expected to follow it.

I now come to another passage in Dr. Mannheim's discussion, which seems to me true. His intellectual integrity prevents him from dissimulating the gloom of our present position; but he succeeds, so far as I can judge, in communicating to most of his readers a feeling of active hopefulness, by infecting them with his own passionate faith in the possibilities of "planning." Yet he says quite clearly:

We have no clear idea how the selection of élites would work in an open mass society in which only the principle of achievement mattered. It is possible that in such a society the succession of the élites would take place much too rapidly, and social continuity which is essentially due to the slow and gradual broadening of the influence of the dominant groups would be lacking in it.[1]

This raises a problem of the first importance to my present discussion, with which I do not think Dr. Mannheim has dealt in any detail: that of the *transmission of culture.*

When we are concerned with the history of certain parts of culture, such as the history of art, or of literature, or of philosophy, we naturally isolate a particular class of phenomena; though there has been a movement, which has produced books of interest and value, to relate these subjects more closely to a general social history. But even such accounts are usually only the history of one class of phenomena interpreted in the light of the history of another class of phenomena and, like that of Dr. Mannheim, tend to take a more limited view of culture than that adopted here. What we have to consider is the parts played by the élite and by the class in the transmission of culture from one generation to the next.

We must remind ourselves of the danger, mentioned in the previous chapter, of identifying culture with the *sum* of distinct cultural activities; and if we avoid this identification we shall also decline to identify our group culture with the sum of the activities of Dr. Mannheim's élites. The anthropologist may study the social system, the economics, the arts, and the religion of a particular tribe, he may even study their psychological peculiarities: but it is not merely by observing in detail all of these manifestations, and grasping them together, that he will approach to an understanding of the culture. For to understand the culture is to understand the people, and this means an imaginative understanding. Such understanding can never be complete: either it is abstract—and the essence escapes—or else it is *lived;* and in so far as it is

---

[1] Dr. Mannheim proceeds to call attention to a tendency in mass-society to renounce even the achievement principle. This passage is important; but as I agree with him that the dangers from this are still more alarming, it is unnecessary to quote it here.

The Class and the Elite

lived, the student will tend to identify himself so completely with the people whom he studies, that he will lose the point of view from which it was worth while and possible to study it. Understanding involves an area more extensive than that of which one can be conscious; one cannot be outside and inside at the same time. What we ordinarily mean by understanding of another people, of course, is an approximation towards understanding which stops short at the point at which the student would begin to lose some essential of his own culture. The man who, in order to understand the inner world of a cannibal tribe, has partaken of the practice of cannibalism, has probably gone too far: he can never quite be one of his own folk again.[1]

I have raised this question, however, solely in support of my contention that culture is not merely the sum of several activities, but a *way of life.* Now the specialist of genius, who may be fully qualified on the ground of his vocational attainment for membership of one of Dr. Mannheim's élites, may very well not be one of the "cultured persons" representative of group culture. As I have said before, he may be only a highly valued contributor to it. Yet group culture, as observable in the past, has never been co-extensive with class, whether an aristocracy or an upper middle class. A very large number of members of these classes always have been conspicuously deficient in "culture." I think that in the past the repository of this culture has been *the* élite, the major part of which was drawn from the dominant class of the time, constituting the primary consumers of the work of thought and art produced by the minority members, who will have originated from various classes, including that class itself. The units of this majority will, some of them, be individuals; others will be families. But the individuals from the dominant class who compose the nucleus of the cultural élite

[1] Joseph Conrad's *Heart of Darkness* gives a hint of something similar.

40

must not thereby be cut off from the class to which they belong, for without their membership of that class they would not have their part to play. It is their function, in relation to the producers, to transmit the culture which they have inherited; just as it is their function, in relation to the rest of their class, to keep it from ossification. It is the function of the class as a whole to preserve and communicate standards of *manners*—which are a vital element in group culture.[1] It is the function of the superior members and superior families to preserve the group culture, as it is the function of the producers to alter it.

In an élite composed of individuals who find their way into it solely for their individual pre-eminence, the differences of background will be so great, that they will be united only by their common interests, and separated by everything else. An élite must therefore be attached to *some* class, whether higher or lower: but so long as there are classes at all it is likely to be the dominant class that attracts this élite to itself. What would happen in a classless society—which is much more difficult to envisage than people think—brings us into the area of conjecture. There are, however, some guesses which seem to me worth venturing.

The primary channel of transmission of culture is the family: no man wholly escapes from the kind, or wholly surpasses the degree, of culture which he acquired from his early environment. It would not do to suggest that this can be the *only* channel of transmission: in a society of any complexity it is supplemented and continued by other conduits of tradition. Even in relatively primitive societies this is so. In more civilised communities of specialised activities, in which not

[1] To avoid misunderstanding at this point, it should be observed that I do not assume that "good manners" should be peculiar to any one stratum of society. In a healthy society, good manners should be found throughout. But as we distinguish between the meanings of "culture" at the several levels, so we distinguish also between the meanings of more and less conscious "good manners."

all the sons would follow the occupation of their father, the apprentice (ideally, at least) did not merely serve his master, and did not merely learn from him as one would learn at a technical school—he became assimilated into a way of life which went with that particular trade or craft; and perhaps the lost secret of the craft is this, that not merely a skill but an entire way of life was transmitted. Culture—distinguishable from knowledge about culture—was transmitted by the older universities: young men have profited there who have been profitless students, and who have acquired no taste for learning, or for Gothic architecture, or for college ritual and form. I suppose that something of the same sort is transmitted also by societies of the masonic type: for initiation is an introduction into a way of life, of however restricted viability, received from the past and to be perpetuated in the future. But by far the most important channel of transmission of culture remains the family: and when family life fails to play its part, we must expect our culture to deteriorate. Now the family is an institution of which nearly everybody speaks well: but it is advisable to remember that this is a term that may vary in extension. In the present age it means little more than the living members. Even of living members, it is a rare exception when an advertisement depicts a large family or three generations: the usual family on the hoardings consists of two parents and one or two young children. What is held up for admiration is not devotion to a family, but personal affection between the members of it: and the smaller the family, the more easily can this personal affection be sentimentalised. But when I speak of the family, I have in mind a bond which embraces a longer period of time than this: a piety towards the dead, however obscure, and a solicitude for the unborn, however remote. Unless this reverence for past and future is cultivated in the home, it can never be more than a verbal convention in the community. Such an interest in the past is different from the vanities and pretensions of genealogy;

such a responsibility for the future is different from that of the builder of social programmes.

I should say then that in a vigorous society there will be both class and élite, with some overlapping and constant interaction between them. An élite, if it is a governing élite, and so far as the natural impulse to pass on to one's offspring both power and prestige is not artificially checked, will tend to establish itself as a class—it is this metamorphosis, I think, which leads to what appears to me an oversight on the part of Dr. Mannheim. But an élite which thus transforms itself tends to lose its function as élite, for the qualities by which the original members won their position will not all be transmitted equally to their descendants. On the other hand, we have to consider what would be the consequence when the converse took place, and we had a society in which the functions of class were assumed by élites. Dr. Mannheim seems to have believed that this will happen; he showed himself, as a passage which I have quoted indicates, aware of the dangers; and he does not appear to have been ready to propose definite safeguards against them.

The situation of a society without classes, and dominated exclusively by élites is, I submit, one about which we have no reliable evidence. By such a society, I suppose we must mean one in which every individual starts without advantage or handicap; and in which, by some mechanism set up by the best designers of such machinery, everybody will find his way, or be directed, to that station of life which he is best fitted to fill, and every position will be occupied by the man or woman best fitted for it. Of course, not even the most sanguine would expect the system to work as well as that: if, by and large, it seemed to come nearer to putting the right people in the right places than any previous system, we should all be satisfied. When I say "dominated," rather than "governed" by élites, I mean that such a society must not be content to be *governed* by the right people: it must see that the ablest artists and architects rise to the top, influence taste, and execute the important public commissions; it must do the same by the other arts and by science; and above all, perhaps, it must be such that the ablest minds will find expression in speculative thought. The system must not only do all this for society in a particular situation—it must *go on* doing it, generation after generation. It would be folly to deny that in a particular phase of a country's development, and *for a limited purpose,* an élite can do a very good job. It may, by expelling a previous governing group, which in contrast to itself may be a *class,* save or reform or revitalise the national life. Such things have happened. But we have very little evidence about the perpetuation of government by élite, and such as we have is unsatisfactory. A considerable time must elapse before we can draw any illustration from Russia. Russia is a rude and vigorous country; it is also a very big country; and it will need a long period of peace and internal development. Three things may happen. Russia may show us how a stable government and a flourishing culture can be transmitted only through élites; it may lapse into oriental lethargy; or the governing élite may follow the course of other governing élites and become a governing class. Nor can we rely upon any evidence from the United States of America. The real revolution in that country was not what is called the Revolution in the history books, but is a consequence of the Civil War; after which arose a plutocratic élite; after which the expansion and material development of the country was accelerated; after which was swollen that stream of mixed immigration, bringing (or rather multiplying) the danger of development into a *caste* system [1] which has not yet been quite dispelled. For the sociologist, the evidence from America is not yet ripe. Our other evidence for government by élite

[1] I believe that the essential difference between a caste and a class system is that the basis of the former is a difference such that the dominant class comes to consider itself a superior *race.*

comes chiefly from France. A governing class, which, during a long period in which the Throne was all-powerful, had ceased to govern, was reduced to the ordinary level of citizenship. Modern France has had no governing class: her political life in the Third Republic, whatever else we may say of it, was *unsettled*. And here we may remark that when a dominant class, however badly it has performed its function, is forcibly removed, its function is not wholly taken over by any other. The "flight of the wild geese" is perhaps a symbol of the harm that England has done to Ireland—more serious, from this point of view, than the massacres of Cromwell, or any of the grievances which the Irish most gladly recall. It may be, too, that England has done more harm to Wales and Scotland by gently attracting their upper classes to certain public schools, than by the wrongs (some real, some imaginary, some misunderstood) voiced by their respective nationalists. But here again, I wish to reserve judgment about Russia. That country, at the time of its revolution, may still have been at so early a stage of its development, that the removal of its upper class may prove not only not to have arrested that development but to have stimulated it. There are, however, some grounds for believing that the elimination of an upper class at a more developed stage can be a disaster for a country: and most certainly when that removal is due to the intervention of another nation.

I have, in the preceding paragraphs, been speaking mainly of the "governing class" and the "governing élite." But I must remind the reader again that in concerning ourselves with class *versus* élite, we are concerned with the total culture of a country, and that involves a good deal more than government. We can yield ourselves with some confidence to a governing élite, as the republican Romans surrendered power to dictators, so long as we have in view a *defined purpose* in a crisis—and a crisis may last a long time. This limited purpose also makes it possible to choose the élite, for we know what we are choosing it for. But, if we are looking for a way to select the right people to constitute every élite, for an indefinite future, by what mechanism are we to do this? If our "purpose" is only to get the best people, in every walk of life, to the top, we lack a criterion of who are the best people; or, if we impose a criterion, it will have an oppressive effect upon novelty. The new work of genius, whether in art, science or philosophy, frequently meets with opposition.

All that concerns me at the moment is the question whether, by education alone, we can ensure the transmission of culture in a society in which some educationists appear indifferent to class distinctions, and from which some other educationists appear to want to remove class distinctions altogether. There is, in any case, a danger of interpreting "education" to cover both too much and too little: too little, when it implies that education is limited to what can be taught; too much, when it implies that everything worth preserving can be transmitted by teaching. In the society desired by some reformers, what the family can transmit will be limited to the minimum, especially if the child is to be, as Mr. H. C. Dent hopes, manipulated by a unified educational system "from the cradle to the grave." And unless the child is classified, by the officials who will have the task of sorting him out, as being just like his father, he will be brought up in a different—not necessarily a better, because all will be equally good, but a different—school environment, and trained on what the official opinion of the moment considers to be "the genuinely democratic lines." The élites, in consequence, will consist solely of individuals whose only common bond will be their professional interest: with no social cohesion, with no social continuity. They will be united only by a part, and that the most conscious part, of their personalities; they will meet like committees. The greater part of their "culture" will be only what they share with all the other individuals composing their nation.

The case for a society with a class structure, the affirmation

46

that it is, in some sense, the "natural" society, is prejudiced
if we allow ourselves to be hypnotised by the two contrasted
terms *aristocracy* and *democracy*. The whole problem is falsi-
fied if we use these terms antithetically. What I have advanced
is not a "defence of aristocracy"—an emphasis upon the importance of one organ of society. Rather it is a plea on behalf
of a form of society in which an aristocracy should have a
peculiar and essential function, as peculiar and essential as
the function of any other part of society. What is important
is a structure of society in which there will be, from "top" to
"bottom," a continuous gradation of cultural levels: it is
important to remember that we should not consider the upper
levels as possessing *more* culture than the lower, but as representing a more conscious culture and a greater specialisation
of culture. I incline to believe that no true democracy can
maintain itself unless it contains these different levels of culture. The levels of culture may also be seen as levels of power,
to the extent that a smaller group at a higher level will have
equal power with a larger group at a lower level; for it may
be argued that complete equality means universal irresponsi-
bility; and in such a society as I envisage, each individual
would inherit greater or less responsibility towards the com-
monwealth, according to the position in society which he inherited—each class would have somewhat different responsi-
bilities. A democracy in which everybody had an equal responsibility in everything would be oppressive for the con-
scientious and licentious for the rest.

There are other grounds upon which a graded society can
be defended; and I hope, in general, that this essay will
suggest lines of thought that I shall not myself explore; but
I must constantly remind the reader of the limits of my subject. If we agree that the primary vehicle for the transmission
of culture is the family, and if we agree that in a more highly
civilised society there must be different levels of culture, then
it follows that to ensure the transmission of the culture of

these different levels there must be groups of families persisting, from generation to generation, each in the same way of life.

And once again I must repeat, that the "conditions of culture" which I set forth do not necessarily produce the higher civilisation: I assert only that when they are absent, the higher civilisation is unlikely to be found.

CHAPTER III

Unity and Diversity: The Region

A diversification among human communities is essential for the provision of the incentive and material for the Odyssey of the human spirit. Other nations of different habits are not enemies: they are godsends. Men require of their neighbours something sufficiently akin to be understood, something sufficiently different to provoke attention, and something great enough to command admiration.

A. N. WHITEHEAD: Science and the Modern World

IT is a recurrent theme of this essay, that a people should be neither too united nor too divided, if its culture is to flourish. Excess of unity may be due to barbarism and may lead to tyranny; excess of division may be due to decadence and may also lead to tyranny: either excess will prevent further development in culture. The proper degree of unity and of diversity cannot be determined for all peoples at all times. We can only state and illustrate some departments in which excess or defect is dangerous: what is necessary, beneficial or deleterious for a particular people at a particular time, must be left to the wisdom of the sage and the insight of the statesman. Neither a classless society, nor a society of strict and impenetrable social barriers is good; each class should have constant additions and defections; the classes, while remaining distinct, should be able to mix freely; and they should all have a community of culture with each other which will give them something in common, more fundamental than the community which each class has with its counterpart in another society. In the previous chapter we considered the special developments of culture by class: we have now to consider the special developments of culture by region.

Of the advantages of administrative and sentimental unity we hardly need to be reminded, after the experience of war; but it is often assumed that the unity of wartime should be preserved in time of peace. Amongst any people engaged in warfare, especially when the war appears, or can be made to appear, purely defensive, we may expect a spontaneous unity of sentiment which is genuine, an affectation of it on the part of those who merely wish to escape odium, and, from all, submission to the commands of the constituted authorities. We should hope to find the same harmony and docility among the survivors of a shipwreck adrift in a lifeboat. People often express regret that the same unity, self-sacrifice and fraternity which prevail in an emergency, cannot survive the emergency itself. Most audiences at Barrie's play, *The Admirable Crichton,* have drawn the inference that the social organisation on the island was right, and that the social organisation at the country seat was wrong: I am not sure that Barrie's play is not susceptible of a different interpretation. We must distinguish at all events between the kind of unity which is necessary in an emergency, and that which is appropriate for the development of culture in a nation at peace. It is conceivable, of course, that a period of "peace" may be a period of preparation for war, or of continuation of warfare in another form: in which situation we may expect a deliberate stimulation of patriotic sentiment and a rigorous central government control. It might be expected, too, in such a period, that "economic warfare" would be conducted by strict government discipline, not left to the guerillas and privateers of enterprise. But I am concerned here with the kind and degree of unity desirable in a country which is at peace with other countries: for if we cannot have periods of real peace, it is futile to hope for culture at all. The kind of unity with which I am concerned is not expressible as a common enthusiasm or a common purpose: enthusiasms and purposes are always transient.

The unity with which I am concerned must be largely unconscious, and therefore can perhaps be best approached through a consideration of the useful diversities. Here I have to do with diversity of region. It is important that a man should feel himself to be, not merely a citizen of a particular nation, but a citizen of a particular part of his country, with local loyalties. These, like loyalty to class, arise out of loyalty to the family. Certainly, an individual may develop the warmest devotion to a place in which he was not born, and to a community with which he has no ancestral ties. But I think we should agree that there would be something artificial, something a little too conscious, about a community of people with strong local feeling, all of whom had come from somewhere else. I think we should say that we must wait for a generation or two for a loyalty which the inhabitants had inherited, and which was not the result of a conscious choice. On the whole, it would appear to be for the best that the great majority of human beings should go on living in the place in which they were born. Family, class and local loyalty all support each other; and if one of these decays, the others will suffer also.

The problem of "regionalism" is seldom contemplated in its proper perspective. I introduce the term "regionalism" deliberately, because of the associations which it is apt to conjure up. It means, I think, to most people, the conception of some small group of local malcontents conducting a political agitation which, because it is not formidable, is regarded as ludicrous—for any movement for what is assumed to be a lost cause always excites ridicule. We expect to find "regionalists" attempting to revive some language which is disappearing and ought to disappear; or to revive customs of a bygone age which have lost all significance; or to obstruct the inevitable and accepted progress of mechanisation and large-scale industry. The champions of local tradition, indeed, often fail to make the best of their case; and when, as sometimes happens, they are most vigorously opposed and derided by others among their own people, the outsider feels that he has no reason to take them seriously. They sometimes misconceive their own case. They are inclined to formulate the remedy wholly in political terms; and as they may be politically inexperienced, and at the same time are agitated by deeper than political motives, their programmes may be patently impracticable. And when they put forward an economic programme, there, too, they are handicapped by having motives which go deeper than economics, in contrast with men who have the reputation of being practical. Furthermore, the usual regionalist is concerned solely with the interests of his own region, and thereby suggests to his neighbour across the border, that what is to the interest of one must be to the disadvantage of the other. The Englishman, for instance, does not ordinarily think of England as a "region" in the way that a Scottish or Welsh national can think of Scotland or Wales; and as it is not made clear to him that his interests also are involved, his sympathies are not enlisted. Thus the Englishman may identify his own interests with a tendency to obliterate local and racial distinctions, which is as harmful to his own culture as to those of his neighbours. Until the case is generalised, therefore, it is not likely to meet with a fair hearing.

At this point the professed regionalist, if he reads these pages, may suspect that I am playing a trick which he sees through. What I am up to, he may think, is trying to deny him the political and economic autonomy of his region, and appease him by offering him a substitute, "cultural autonomy," which, because it is divorced from political and economic power, will only be a shadow of the real thing. I am quite aware that the political, the economic and the cultural problems cannot be isolated from each other. I am quite aware that any local "cultural revival" which left the political and economic framework unaffected, would hardly be more than an artificially sustained antiquarianism: what is wanted is not to restore a vanished, or to revive a vanishing culture under modern conditions which make it impossible, but to grow a contemporary culture from the old roots. But the political and economic conditions of healthy regionalism are not the concern of the present essay; nor are they matters on which I am qualified to pronounce. Nor, I think, should the political or the economic problem be the *primary* concern of the true regionalist. The *absolute* value is that each area should have its characteristic culture, which should also harmonise with, and enrich, the cultures of the neighbouring areas. In order to realise this value it is necessary to investigate political and economic alternatives to centralisation in London or elsewhere: and here, it is a question of the possible—of what can be done which will support this absolute value of culture, without injury to the island as a whole and by consequence to that part of it also in which the regionalist is interested. But this is beyond my scope.

We are, you will have noticed, primarily concerned with the particular constellation of cultures which is found in the British Isles. The clearest among the differences to be considered is that of the areas which still possess languages of their own. Even this division is not so simple as it looks: for a people (like the English-speaking Irish) which has lost its language may preserve enough of the structure, idiom, intonation and rhythm of its original tongue (vocabulary is of minor importance) for its speech and writing to have qualities not elsewhere found in the language of its adoption. And on the other hand a "dialect" may preserve the vestiges, on the lowest level of culture, of a variety of the language which once had equal status with any. But the unmistakable *satellite* culture is one which preserves its language, but which is so closely associated with, and dependent upon, another, that not only certain classes of the population, but all of them, have to be bi-lingual. It differs from the culture of the independent small nation in this respect, that in the latter it is usually only necessary for some classes to know another language; and in the independent small nation, those who need to know one foreign language are likely to need two or three: so that the pull towards one foreign culture will be balanced by the attraction of at least one other. A nation of weaker culture may be under the influence of one or another stronger culture at different periods: a true satellite culture is one which, for geographical and other reasons, has a permanent relation to a stronger one.

When we consider what I call the satellite culture, we find two reasons against consenting to its complete absorption into the stronger culture. The first objection is one so profound that it must simply be accepted: it is the instinct of every living thing to persist in its own being. The resentment against absorption is sometimes most strongly felt, and most loudly voiced, by those individuals in whom it is united with an unacknowledged awareness of inferiority or failure; and on the other hand it is often repudiated by those individuals for whom adoption into the stronger culture has meant success—greater power, prestige or wealth than could have been theirs had their fortunes been circumscribed by their area of origin.[1] But when the testimony of both these types of individual has been discounted, we may say that any vigorous small people wants to preserve its individuality.

The other reason for the preservation of local culture is one which is also a reason for the satellite culture continuing

[1] It is not unknown, however, that the successful self-exile sometimes manifests an exaggerated sentiment towards his native region, to which he may return for his holidays, or to enjoy the affluent retirement of his declining years.

to be satellite, and not going so far as to try to cut itself off completely. It is that the satellite exercises a considerable influence upon the stronger culture; and so plays a larger part in the world at large than it could in isolation. For Ireland, Scotland and Wales to cut themselves off completely from England would be to cut themselves off from Europe and the world, and no talk of auld alliances would help matters. But it is the other side of the question that interests me more, for it is the side that has received less acknowledgment. It is that the survival of the satellite culture is of very great value to the stronger culture. It would be no gain whatever for English culture, for the Welsh, Scots and Irish to become indistinguishable from Englishmen—what *would* happen, of course, is that we should all become indistinguishable featureless "Britons," at a lower lever of culture than that of any of the separate regions. On the contrary, it is of great advantage for English culture to be constantly influenced from Scotland, Ireland and Wales.

A people is judged by history according to its contribution to the culture of other peoples flourishing at the same time and according to its contribution to the cultures which arise afterwards. It is from this point of view that I look at the question of the preservation of languages—I am not interested in languages in an advanced state of decay (that is to say, when they are no longer adequate to the needs of expression of the more educated members of the community). It is sometimes considered an advantage, and a source of glory, that one's own language should be a necessary medium for as many foreigners as possible: I am not sure that this popularity is without grave dangers for any language. A less dubious advantage of certain languages which are native to large numbers of people, is that they have become, because of the work done by scientists and philosophers who have thought in those languages, and because of the traditions thus created, better vehicles than others for scientific and abstract thought. The case for the more restricted languages must be put on grounds which have less immediate appeal.

The question we may ask about such a language as Welsh, is whether it is of any value to the world at large, that it should be used in Wales. But this is really as much as to ask whether the Welsh, *qua* Welsh, are of any use? not, of course, as human beings, but as the preservers and continuers of a culture which is not English. The direct contribution to poetry by Welshmen and men of Welsh extraction, writing in English, is very considerable; and considerable also is the influence of their poetry upon poets of different racial origins. The fact that an extensive amount of poetry has been written in the Welsh language, in the ages when the English language was unknown in Wales, is of less direct importance: for there appears no reason why this should not be studied by those who will take the trouble to learn the language, on the same terms as poetry written in Latin or Greek. On the surface, there would seem to be every reason why Welsh poets should compose in the English language exclusively: for I know of no instance of a poet having reached the first rank in both languages; and the Welsh influence upon English poetry has been the work chiefly of Welsh poets who wrote only in English. But it must be remembered, that for the transmission of a culture—a peculiar way of thinking, feeling and behaving— and for its maintenance, there is no safeguard more reliable than a language. And to survive for this purpose it must continue to be a literary language—not necessarily a scientific language but certainly a poetic one: otherwise the spread of education will extinguish it. The literature written in that language will not, of course, make any direct impact upon the world at large; but if it is no longer cultivated, the people to whom it belongs (we are considering particularly the Welsh) will tend to lose their racial character. The Welsh will be less Welsh; and their poets will cease to have any contribution to make to English literature, beyond their individual genius.

And I am of opinion, that the benefits which Scottish, Welsh and Irish writers have conferred upon English literature are far in excess of what the contribution of all these individual men of genius would have been had they, let us say, all been adopted in early infancy by English foster-parents.

I am not concerned, in an essay which aims at least at the merit of brevity, to defend the thesis, that it is desirable that the English should continue to be English. I am obliged to take that for granted: and if this assumption is called into question, I must defend it on another occasion. But if I can defend with any success the thesis, that it is to the advantage of England that the Welsh should continue to be Welsh, the Scots Scots and the Irish Irish, then the reader should be disposed to agree that there may be some advantage to other peoples in the English continuing to be English. It is an essential part of my case, that if the other cultures of the British Isles were wholly superseded by English culture, English culture would disappear too. Many people seem to take for granted that English culture is something self-sufficient and secure; that it will persist whatever happens. While some refuse to admit that any foreign influence can be bad, others assume complacently that English culture could flourish in complete isolation from the Continent. To many it has never occurred to reflect that the disappearance of the peripheral cultures of England (to say nothing of the more humble local peculiarities within England itself) might be a calamity. We have not given enough attention to the ecology of cultures. It is probable, I think, that complete uniformity of culture throughout these islands would bring about a lower grade of culture altogether.

It should be clear that I attempt no solution of the regional problem; and the "solution" would have in any case to vary indefinitely according to local needs and possibilities. I am trying only to take apart, and leave to others to reassemble, the elements in the problem. I neither support nor dispute

57

any specific proposals for particular regional reforms. Most attempts to solve the problem seem to me to suffer from a failure to examine closely either the unity, or the differences, between the cultural, political and economic aspects. To deal with one of these aspects, to the exclusion of the others, is to produce a programme which will, because of its inadequacy, appear a little absurd. If the nationalistic motive in regionalism were pushed very far, it certainly would lead to absurdity. The close association of the Bretons with the French, and of the Welsh with the English, is to the advantage of everybody: an association of Brittany and Wales which ruptured their connexions with France and England respectively, would be an unqualified misfortune. For a national culture, if it is to flourish, should be a constellation of cultures, the constituents of which, benefiting each other, benefit the whole.

At this point I introduce a new notion: that of the vital importance for a society of *friction* between its parts. Accustomed as we are to think in figures of speech taken from machinery, we assume that a society, like a machine, should be as well oiled as possible, provided with ball bearings of the best steel. We think of friction as waste of energy. I shall not attempt to substitute any other imagery: perhaps at this point the less we think in analogies the better. In the last chapter I suggested that in any society which became permanently established in either a caste or a classless system, the culture would decay: one might even put it that a classless society should always be emerging into class, and a class society should be tending towards obliteration of its class distinctions. I now suggest that both class and region, by dividing the inhabitants of a country into two different kinds of groups, lead to a conflict favourable to creativeness and progress. And (to remind the reader of what I said in my introduction) these are only two of an indefinite number of conflicts and jealousies which should be profitable to society. Indeed, the more the better: so that everyone should be an ally of everyone else in some respects, and an opponent in several others, and no one conflict, envy or fear will dominate.

As individuals, we find that our development depends upon the people whom we meet in the course of our lives. (These people include the authors whose books we read, and characters in works of fiction and history.) The benefit of these meetings is due as much to the differences as to the resemblances; to the conflict, as well as the sympathy, between persons. Fortunate the man who, at the right moment, meets the right friend; fortunate also the man who at the right moment meets the right enemy. I do not approve the extermination of the enemy: the policy of exterminating or, as is barbarously said, liquidating enemies, is one of the most alarming developments of modern war and peace, from the point of view of those who desire the survival of culture. One needs the enemy. So, within limits, the friction, not only between individuals but between groups, seems to me quite necessary for civilisation. The universality of irritation is the best assurance of peace. A country within which the divisions have gone too far is a danger to itself: a country which is too well united—whether by nature or by device, by honest purpose or by fraud and oppression—is a menace to others. In Italy and in Germany, we have seen that a unity with politico-economic aims, imposed violently and too rapidly, had unfortunate effects upon both nations. Their cultures had developed in the course of a history of extreme, and extremely sub-divided regionalism: the attempt to teach Germans to think of themselves as Germans first, and the attempt to teach Italians to think of themselves as Italians first, rather than as natives of a particular small principality or city, was to disturb the traditional culture from which alone any future culture could grow.

I may put the idea of the importance of conflict within a nation more positively, by insisting on the importance of various and sometimes conflicting loyalties. If we consider these two divisions alone, of class and region, these ought to some extent to operate against each other: a man should have certain interests and sympathies in common with other men of the same local culture as against those of his own class elsewhere; and interests and sympathies in common with others of his class, irrespective of place. Numerous cross-divisions favour peace within a nation, by dispersing and confusing animosities; they favour peace between nations, by giving every man enough antagonism at home to exercise all his aggressiveness. The majority of men commonly dislike foreigners, and are easily inflamed against them; and it is not possible for the majority to know much about foreign peoples. A nation which has gradations of class seems to me, other things being equal, likely to be more tolerant and pacific than one which is not so organised.

So far, we have proceeded from the greater to the less, finding a national culture to be the resultant of an indefinite number of local cultures which, when themselves analysed, are composed of still smaller local cultures. Ideally, each village, and of course more visibly the larger towns, should have each its peculiar character. But I have already suggested that a national culture is the better for being in contact with outside cultures, both giving and receiving: and we shall now proceed in the opposite direction, from the smaller to the larger. As we go in this direction, we find that the content of the term *culture* undergoes some change: the word *means* something rather different, if we are speaking of the culture of a village, of a small region, of an island like Britain which comprehends several distinct racial cultures; and the meaning is altered much more when we come to speak of "European culture." We have to abandon most of the political associations, for whereas in such smaller units of culture as I have just mentioned there is normally a certain unity of government, the unity of government of the Holy Roman Empire was, throughout most of the period covered by the term, both precarious and largely nominal. Of the nature of the unity of culture in Western Europe, I have written in the three broadcast talks—composed for another audience and therefore in a somewhat different style from the body of this essay—which I have added as an appendix under the title of "The Unity of European Culture." I shall not attempt to cover the same ground in this chapter, but shall proceed to enquire what meaning, if any, can be attached to the term "world culture." The investigation of a possible "world culture" should be of particular interest to those who champion any of the various schemes for world-federation, or for a world government: for, obviously, so long as there exist cultures which are beyond some point antagonistic to each other, antagonistic to the point of irreconcilability, all attempts at politico-economic unification will be in vain. I say "beyond some point," because in the relations of any two cultures there will be two opposite forces balancing each other: attraction and repulsion—without the attraction they could not affect each other, and without the repulsion they could not survive as distinct cultures; one would absorb the other, or both would be fused into one culture. Now the zealots of world-government seem to me sometimes to assume, unconsciously, that their unity of organisation has an absolute value, and that if differences between cultures stand in the way, these must be abolished. If these zealots are of the humanitarian type, they will assume that this process will take place naturally and painlessly: they may, without knowing it, take for granted that the final world-culture will be simply an extension of that to which they belong themselves. Our Russian friends, who are more realistic, if not in the long run any more practical, are much more conscious of irreconcilability between cultures; and appear to hold the view that any culture incompatible with their own should be forcibly uprooted.

The world-planners who are both serious and humane, however, might—if we believed that their methods would succeed—be as grave a menace to culture as those who practise more violent methods. For it must follow from what I have already pleaded about the value of local cultures, that a world culture which was simply a *uniform* culture would be no culture at all. We should have a humanity de-humanised. It would be a nightmare. But on the other hand, we cannot resign the idea of world-culture altogether. For if we content ourselves with the ideal of "European culture" we shall still be unable to fix any definite frontiers. European culture has an area, but no definite frontiers: and you cannot build Chinese walls. The notion of a purely self-contained European culture would be as fatal as the notion of a self-contained national culture: in the end as absurd as the notion of preserving a local uncontaminated culture in a single county or village of England. We are therefore pressed to maintain the ideal of a world culture, while admitting that it is something we cannot *imagine*. We can only conceive it, as the logical term of relations between cultures. Just as we recognise that the parts of Britain must have in one sense, a common culture, though this common culture is only actual in diverse local manifestations, so we must aspire to a common world culture, which will yet not diminish the particularity of the constituent parts. And here, of course, we are finally up against religion, which so far, in the consideration of local differences within the same area, we have not had to face. Ultimately, antagonistic religions must mean antagonistic cultures; and ultimately, religions cannot be reconciled. From the official Russian point of view there are two objections to religion: first, of course, that religion is apt to provide another loyalty than that claimed by the State; and second, that there are several religions in the world still firmly maintained by many believers. The second objection is perhaps even more serious than the first: for where there is only one religion, it is always possible that that religion may be subtly altered, so that it will enjoin conformity rather than stimulate resistance to the State.

We are the more likely to be able to stay loyal to the ideal of the unimaginable world culture, if we recognise all the difficulties, the practical impossibility, of its realisation. And there are further difficulties which cannot be ignored. We have so far considered cultures as if they had all come into being by the same process of growth: the same people in the same place. But there is the *colonial* problem, and the *colonisation* problem: it is a pity that the world "colony" has had to do duty for two quite different meanings. The colonial problem is that of the relation between an indigenous native culture and a foreign culture, when a higher foreign culture has been imposed, often by force, upon a lower. This problem is insoluble, and takes several forms. There is one problem when we come into contact with a lower culture for the first time: there are very few places in the world where this is still possible. There is another problem where a native culture has already begun to disintegrate under foreign influence, and where a native population has already taken in more of the foreign culture than it can ever expel. There is a third problem where, as in some of the West Indies, several uprooted peoples have been haphazardly mixed. And these problems are insoluble, in the sense that, whatever we do towards their solution or mitigation, we do not altogether know what we are doing. We must be aware of them; we must do what we can, so far as our understanding will take us; but many more forces enter into the changes of the culture of a people than we can grasp and control; and any positive and excellent development of culture is always a miracle when it happens.

The colonisation problem arises from migration. When peoples migrated across Asia and Europe in pre-historic and early times, it was a whole tribe, or at least a wholly representative part of it, that moved together. Therefore, it was a total culture that moved. In the migrations of modern times, the emigrants have come from countries already highly civilised. They came from countries where the development of social organisation was already complex. The people who migrated have never represented the whole of the culture of the country from which they came, or they have represented it in quite different proportions. They have transplanted themselves according to some social, religious, economic or political determination, or some peculiar mixture of these. There has therefore been something in the removements analogous in nature to religious schism. The people have taken with them only a part of the total culture in which, so long as they remained at home, they participated. The culture which develops on the new soil must therefore be bafflingly alike and different from the parent culture: it will be complicated sometimes by whatever relations are established with some native race, and further by immigration from other than the original source. In this way, peculiar types of culture-sympathy and culture-clash appear, between the areas populated by colonisation and the countries of Europe from which the migrants came.

There is finally the peculiar case of India, where almost every complication is found to defeat the culture-planner. There is stratification of society which is not purely social but to some extent racial, in a Hindu world which comprehends peoples with an ancient tradition of high civilisation, and tribesmen of very primitive culture indeed. There is Brahminism and there is Islam. There are two or more important cultures on completely different religious foundations. Into this confused world came the British, with their assurance that their own culture was the best in the world, their ignorance of the relation between culture and religion, and (at least since the nineteenth century) their bland assumption that religion was a secondary matter. It is human, when we do not understand another human being, and cannot ignore him, to exert an unconscious pressure on that person to turn him into something that we *can* understand: many husbands and wives exert this pressure on each other. The effect on the person so influenced is liable to be the repression and distortion, rather than the improvement, of the personality; and no man is good enough to have the right to make another over in his own image. The benefits of British rule will soon be lost, but the ill effects of the disturbance of a native culture by an alien one will remain. To offer another people your culture first, and your religion second, is a reversal of values: and while every European represents, for good or ill, the culture to which he belongs, only a small minority are worthy representatives of its religious faith.[1] The only prospect of stability in India seems the alternative of a development, let us hope under peaceful conditions, into a loose federation of kingdoms, or to a mass uniformity attainable only at the price of the abolition of class distinctions and the abandonment of all religion—which would mean the disappearance of Indian culture.

I have thought it necessary to make this brief excursion into the several types of culture relation between one nation and the different kinds of foreign area, because the regional problem within the nation has to be seen in this larger context. There can be, of course, no one simple solution. As I have said, the improvement and transmission of culture can never be the direct object of any of our practical activities: all we can do is to try to keep in mind that whatever we do will affect our own culture or that of some other people. We can also learn to respect every other culture as a whole, however inferior to our own it may appear, or however justly we may disapprove of some features of it: the deliberate

[1] It is interesting to speculate, even though we cannot prove our conclusions, what would have happened to Western Europe had the Roman conquest imposed a culture pattern which left the religious beliefs and practices unaffected.

destruction of another culture as a whole is an irreparable wrong, almost as evil as to treat human beings like animals. But it is when we give our attention to the question of unity and diversity within the limited area that we know best, and within which we have the most frequent opportunities for right action, that we can combat the hopelessness that invades us, when we linger too long upon perplexities so far beyond our measure.

It was necessary to remind ourselves of those considerable areas of the globe, in which the problem takes a different form from ours: of those areas particularly, in which two or more distinct cultures are so inextricably involved with each other, in propinquity and in the ordinary business of living, that "regionalism," as we conceive it in Britain, would be a mockery. For such areas it is probable that a very different type of political philosophy should inspire political action, from that in terms of which we are accustomed to think and act in this part of the world. It is as well to have these differences at the back of our mind, that we may appreciate better the conditions with which we have to deal at home. These conditions are those of a homogeneous general culture, associated with the traditions of one religion: given these conditions, we can maintain the conception of a national culture which will draw its vitality from the cultures of its several areas, within each of which again there will be smaller units of culture having their own local peculiarities.

CHAPTER IV

Unity and Diversity: Sect and Cult

IN the first chapter I tried to place myself at a point of view from which the same phenomena appear both religious and cultural. In this chapter I shall be concerned with the cultural significance of religious divisions. While the considerations put forward should, if worthy of being taken seriously, have a particular interest for those Christians who are perplexed over the problem of Christian reunion, they are primarily intended to show that Christian divisions, and therefore schemes for Christian reunion, should be of concern not only to Christians, but to everybody except those who advocate a kind of society which would break completely with the Christian tradition.

I asserted, in the first chapter, that in the most primitive societies no clear distinction is visible between religious and non-religious activities; and that as we proceed to examine the more developed societies, we perceive a greater distinction, and finally contrast and opposition, between these activities. The sort of identity of religion and culture which we observe amongst peoples of very low development cannot recur except in the New Jerusalem. A higher religion is one which is much more difficult to believe. For the more conscious becomes the belief, so the more conscious becomes unbelief: indifference, doubt and scepticism appear, and the endeavour to adapt the tenets of religion to what people in each age find easiest to believe. In the higher religion, it is more difficult also to make behaviour conform to the moral laws of the religion. A higher religion imposes a conflict, a division, torment and struggle within the individual; a conflict sometimes between the laity and the priesthood; a conflict eventually between Church and State.

The reader may have difficulty in reconciling these assertions with the point of view set forth in my first chapter, according to which there is always, even in the most conscious and highly developed societies that we know, an aspect of identity between the religion and the culture. I wish to maintain *both* these points of view. We do not leave the earlier stage of development behind us: it is that upon which we build. The identity of religion and culture remains on the unconscious level, upon which we have superimposed a conscious structure wherein religion and culture are contrasted and can be opposed. The *meaning* of the terms "religion" and "culture" is of course altered between these two levels. To the unconscious level we constantly tend to revert, as we find consciousness an excessive burden; and the tendency towards reversion may explain the powerful attraction which totalitarian philosophy and practice can exert upon humanity. Totalitarianism appeals to the desire to return to the womb. The contrast between religion and culture imposes a strain: we escape from this strain by attempting to revert to an identity of religion and culture which prevailed at a more primitive stage; as when we indulge in alcohol as an anodyne, we consciously seek unconsciousness. It is only by unremitting effort that we can persist in being individuals in a society, instead of merely members of a disciplined crowd. Yet we remain members of the crowd, even when we succeed in being individuals. Hence, for the purposes of this essay, I am obliged to maintain two contradictory propositions: that religion and culture are aspects of one unity, and that they are two different and contrasted things.

I attempt, as far as possible, to contemplate my problems from the point of view of the sociologist, and not from that of the Christian apologist. Most of my generalisations are intended to have some applicability to all religion, and not only to Christianity; and when, as in what follows in this chapter, I discuss Christian matters, that is because I am particularly concerned with Christian culture, with the Western World, with Europe, and with England. In saying that I aim at taking, as consistently as I can, the sociological point of view, I must make clear that I do not think that the difference between the religious and the sociological point of view is so easily maintained as the difference between a couple of adjectives might lead us to suppose. We may here define the religious point of view, as that from which we ask the question, whether the tenets of a religion are true or false. It follows that we shall be taking the religious point of view, if we are atheists whose thinking is based on the assumption that all religions are untrue. From the sociological point of view, the truth or falsity is irrelevant: we are concerned only with the comparative effects of different religious structures upon culture. Now, if students of the subject could be neatly divided into theologians, including atheists, and sociologists, the problem would be very different from what it is. But, for one thing, no religion can be wholly "understood" from the out-side—even the sociologist's purposes. For another, no one can wholly escape the religious point of view, because in the end one either believes or disbelieves. Therefore, no one can be as wholly detached and disinterested as the ideal sociologist should be. The reader accordingly must try, not only to make allowance for the religious views of the author, but, what is more difficult, to make allowance for his own—and he may never have examined thoroughly his own mind. So both writer and reader must be on guard against assuming that they are wholly detached.[1]

We have now to consider unity and diversity in religious belief and practice, and enquire what is the situation most favourable to the preservation and improvement of culture. I have suggested in my first chapter that those among the "higher religions" which are most likely to continue to stimulate culture, are those which are capable of being accepted by peoples of different cultures: those which have the greatest universality—though potential universality by itself may be no criterion of a "higher religion." Such religions can provide a ground pattern of common belief and behaviour, upon which a variety of local patterns can be embroidered; and they will encourage a reciprocal influence of peoples upon each other, such that any cultural progress in one area may quicken development in another. In certain historical conditions, a fierce exclusiveness may be a necessary condition for the preservation of a culture: the Old Testament bears witness to this.[2] In spite of this particular historical situation, we should be able to agree that the practice of a common religion, by peoples each having its own cultural character, should usually promote the exchange of influence to their reciprocal advantage. It is of course conceivable that a religion may be too easily accommodated to a variety of cultures, and become assimilated without assimilating; and that this weakness may tend to bring about the opposite result, if the religion breaks

[1] See a valuable article by Professor Evans-Pritchard on "Social Anthropology" in *Blackfriars* for November 1946. He remarks: "The answer would seem to be that the sociologist should also be a moral philosopher and that, as such, he should have a set of definite beliefs and values in terms of which he evaluates the facts he studies as a sociologist."

[2] Since the diaspora, and the scattering of Jews amongst peoples holding the Christian Faith, it may have been unfortunate both for these peoples and for the Jews themselves, that the culture-contact between them has had to be within those neutral zones of culture in which religion could be ignored: and the effect may have been to strengthen the illusion that there can be culture without religion.

up into branches or sects so opposed that they cease to influence each other. Christianity and Buddhism have been exposed to this danger.

From this point it is with Christianity alone that I am to be concerned; in particular with the relation of Catholicism and Protestantism in Europe and the diversity of sects within Protestantism. We must try to start without any bias for, or against, unity or reunion or the maintenance of the separate corporate identity of religious denominations. We must take note of whatever injury appears to have been done to European culture, and to the culture of any part of Europe, by division into sects. On the other hand, we must acknowledge that many of the most remarkable achievements of culture have been made since the sixteenth century, in conditions of disunity: and that some, indeed, as in nineteenth-century France, appear after the religious foundations for culture seem to have crumbled away. We cannot affirm that if the religious unity of Europe had continued, these or equally brilliant achievements would have been realised. Either religious unity or religious division may coincide with cultural efflorescence or cultural decay.

From this point of view, we may take a moderate satisfaction, which should not be allowed to settle into complacency, when we review the history of England. In a nation in which no *tendency* to Protestantism appeared, or in which it was negligible, there must always be a danger of religious petrifaction, and of aggressive unbelief. In a nation in which the relations of Church and State run too smoothly, it does not matter much, from our present point of view, whether the cause is ecclesiasticism, the dominance of State by Church, or erastianism, the dominance of Church by State. Indeed, it is not always easy to distinguish between the two conditions. The effect equally may be, that every disaffected person, and every sufferer from injustice, will attribute his misfortunes to the inherent evil of the Church, or to an inherent evil in Christianity itself. Formal obedience to the Roman See is itself no assurance that, in a wholly Catholic nation, religion and culture will not become too closely identified. Elements of local culture—even of local barbarism—may become invested with the sanctity of religious observances, and superstition may flourish under the guise of piety: a people may tend to slip back towards the unity of religion and culture that pertains to primitive communities. The result of the unquestioned dominance of one cult, when a people is passive, may be torpor: when a people is quick and self-assertive, the result may be chaos. For, as discontent turns to disaffection, the anti-clerical bias may become an anti-religious tradition; a distinct and hostile culture grows and flourishes, and a nation is divided against itself. The factions have to continue to live with each other; and the common language and ways of life which they retain, far from mollifying animosity, may only exasperate it. The religious division becomes a symbol for a group of associated differences, often rationally unrelated; around these differences swarm a host of private grievances, fears and interests; and the contest for an indivisible heritage may terminate only in exhaustion.

It would here be irrelevant to review those sanguinary passages of civil strife, such as the Thirty Years War, in which Catholics and Protestants fought over such an heritage. Explicit theological contentions between Christians no longer attract to themselves those other irreconcilable interests which seek a decision by arms. The deepest causes of division may still be religious, but they become conscious, not in theological but in political, social and economic doctrines. Certainly, in those countries in which the prevailing faith has been Protestant, anti-clericalism seldom takes a violent form. In such countries, both faith and infidelity tend to be mild and inoffensive; as the culture has become secularised, the cultural differences between faithful and infidel are minimal; the boundary between belief and unbelief is vague; the Christianity is more pliant, the atheism more negative; and all parties live in amity, so long as they continue to accept some common moral conventions.

The situation in England, however, differs from that in other countries, whether Catholic or Protestant. In England, as in other Protestant countries, atheism has been mostly of a passive kind. No statistician could produce an estimate of the numbers of Christians and non-Christians. Many people live on an unmarked frontier enveloped in dense fog; and those who dwell beyond it are more numerous in the dark waste of ignorance and indifference, than in the well-lighted desert of atheism. The English unbeliever, of some social status however humble, is likely to conform to the practices of Christianity on the occasions of birth, death and the first venture in matrimony. Atheists in this country are not yet culturally united: their types of atheism will vary according to the culture of the religious communion in which they, or their parents, or their grandparents were reared. The chief cultural differences in England have, in the past, been those between Anglicanism and the more important Protestant sects; and even these differences are far from clearly defined: first, because the Church of England itself has comprehended wider variations of belief and cult than a foreign observer would believe it possible for one institution to contain without bursting; and second, because of the number and variety of the sects separated from it.

If my contentions in the first chapter are accepted, it will be agreed that the formation of a religion is also the formation of a culture. From this it should follow that, as a religion divides into sects, and as these sects develop from generation to generation, a variety of cultures will be propagated. And, as the intimacy of religion and culture is such that we may expect what happens one way to happen the other, we are prepared to find that the division between Christian cultures will stimulate further differentiations of belief and cult. It does not fall within my purpose to consider the Great Schism between East and West which corresponds to the shifting geographical boundary between two cultures. When we consider the Western World, we must recognise that the main cultural tradition has been that corresponding to the Church of Rome. Only within the last four hundred years has any other manifested itself; and anyone with a sense of centre and periphery must admit that the western tradition has been Latin, and Latin means Rome. There are countless testimonies of art and thought and manners; and among these we must include the work of all men born and educated in a Catholic society, whatever their individual beliefs. From this point of view, the separation of Northern Europe, and of England in particular, from communion with Rome represents a diversion from the main stream of culture. To pronounce, upon this separation, any judgment of value, to assume that it was a good or a bad thing, is what in this investigation we must try to avoid; for that would be to pass from the sociological to the theological point of view. And as I must at this point introduce the term *sub-culture* to signify the culture which pertains to the area of a divided part of Christendom, we must be careful not to assume that a sub-culture is necessarily an inferior culture; remembering also that while a sub-culture may suffer loss in being separated from the main body, the main body may also be mutilated by the loss of a member of itself.

We must recognise next, that where a sub-culture has in time become established as the main culture *of a particular territory,* it tends to change places, for that territory, with the main European culture. In this respect it differs from those sub-cultures representing sects the members of which share a region with the main culture. In England, the main cultural tradition has for several centuries been Anglican. Roman Catholics in England are, of course, in a more central European tradition than are Anglicans; yet, because the main tradition of England has been Anglican, they are in another aspect more outside of the tradition than are Protestant dissenters. It is Protestant dissent which is, in relation to Anglicanism, a congeries of sub-cultures: or, when we regard Anglicanism itself as a sub-culture, we might refer to it as a congeries of "sub-sub-cultures"—as this term is too clownish to be admitted into good company, we can only say "secondary sub-cultures." By Protestant dissent I mean those bodies which recognise each other as "the Free Churches," together with the Society of Friends, which has an isolated but distinguished history: all minor religious entities are culturally negligible. The variations of character among the chief religious bodies, have to some extent to do with the peculiar circumstances of their origins, and the length of the separation. It is of some interest that Congregationalism, which has a long history, numbers several distinguished theologians; whereas Methodism, with a briefer history, and less theological justification for its separate existence, appears to rely chiefly on its hymnology, and to need no independent theological structure of its own. But whether we consider a territorial sub-culture, or a secondary sub-culture within a territory or scattered over several territories, we may find ourselves led to the conclusion, that every sub-culture is dependent upon that from which it is an offshoot. The life of Protestantism depends upon the survival of that against which it protests; and just as the culture of Protestant dissent would perish of inanition without the persistence of Anglican culture, so the maintenance of English culture is contingent upon the health of the culture of Latin Europe, and upon continuing to draw sustenance from that Latin culture.

There is, however, a difference between the division of Canterbury from Rome, and the division of Free Protestantism from Canterbury, which is important for my purposes. It corresponds to a difference presented in the previous chapter, between colonisation by mass migration (as in the early movements westwards across Europe) and colonisation by cer-

tain elements separating themselves from a culture which remains at home (as in the colonisation of the Dominions and
the Americas). The separation precipitated by Henry VIII
had the immediate cause of personal motives in high quarters;
it was reinforced by tendencies strong in England and in
Northern Europe, of more respectable origin. Once released,
the forces of Protestantism went further than Henry himself
intended or would have approved. But, although the Reformation in England was, like any other revolution, the work of a
minority, and although it met with several local movements
of stubborn resistance, it eventually carried with it the greater
part of the nation irrespective of class or region. The Protestant sects, on the other hand, represent certain elements in
English culture to the exclusion of others: class and occupation played a large part in their formation. It would probably be impossible for the closest student to pronounce how
far it is adherence to dissenting tenets that forms a sub-culture,
and how far it is the formation of a sub-culture that inspires
the finding of reasons for dissent. The solution of that enigma
is fortunately not necessary for my purpose. The result, in any
case, was a stratification of England by sects, in some measure
proceeding from, in some measure aggravating, the cultural
distinctions between classes.

It might be possible for a profound student of ethnology
and of the history of early settlement in this island, to argue
the existence of causes of a more stubborn and more primitive nature, for the tendencies to religious fission. He might
trace them to ineradicable differences between the culture
of the several tribes, races and languages which from time
to time held sway or contested for supremacy. He might,
furthermore, take the view that cultural mixture does not
necessarily follow the same course as biological mixture; and
that, even if we assumed every person of purely English
descent to have the blood of all the successive invaders
mingled in his veins in exactly the same proportions, it need

not follow that cultural fusion ensued. He might therefore discover, in the tendency of various elements in the population to express their faith in different ways, to prefer different types of communal organisation and different styles of worship, a reflection of early divisions between dominant and subject races. Such speculations, which I am too unlearned to support or oppose, lie outside of my scope; but it is as well for both writer and readers to remind themselves that there may be deeper levels than that upon which the enquiry is being conducted. If differences persisting to the present day could be established in descent from primitive differences of culture, this would only reinforce the case for the unity of religion and culture propounded in my first chapter.

However this may be, there are curiosities enough to occupy our attention in the mixture of motives and interests in the dissensions of religious parties within the period of modern history. One need not be a cynic to be amused, or a devotee to be saddened, by the spectacle of the self-deception, as well as the frequent hypocrisy, of the attackers and defenders of one or another form of the Christian Faith. But from the point of view of my essay, both mirth and sorrow are irrelevant, because this confusion is just what one must expect, being inherent in the human condition. There are, certainly, situations in history in which a religious contest can be attributed to a purely religious motive. The life-long battle of St. Athanasius against the Arians and Eutychians need not be regarded in any other light than the light of theology: the scholar who endeavoured to demonstrate that it represented a culture-clash between Alexandria and Antioch, or some similar ingenuity, would appear to us at best to be talking about something else. Even the purest theological issue, however, will in the long run have cultural consequences: a superficial acquaintance with the career of Athanasius should be enough to assure us that he was one of the great builders of western civilisation. And, for the most part, it is *inevitable* that we should, when we defend our religion, be defending at the same time our culture, and vice versa: we are obeying the fundamental instinct to preserve our existence. And in so doing, in the course of time we make many errors and commit many crimes—most of which may be simplified into the one error, of identifying our religion and our culture on a level on which we ought to distinguish them from each other.

Such considerations are relevant not only to the history of religious strife and separation: they are equally pertinent when we come to entertain schemes for reunion. The importance of stopping to examine cultural peculiarities, to disentangle religious from cultural hindrances, has hitherto been overlooked—and I should say more than overlooked: deliberately though unconsciously ignored—in the schemes of reunion between Christian bodies adopted or put forward. Hence the appearance of disingenuousness, of agreement upon formulae to which the contracting parties can give different interpretations, which provokes a comparison with treaties between governments.

The reader unacquainted with the details of "oecumenicity," should be reminded of the difference between *inter-communion* and *reunion*. An arrangement of inter-communion between two national churches—such as the Church of England and the Church of Sweden—or between the Church of England and one of the Eastern Churches, or between the Church of England and a body such as the "Old Catholics" found in Holland and elsewhere on the Continent, does not necessarily look any further than what the term implies: a reciprocal recognition of the "validity of orders" and of the orthodoxy of tenets; with the consequence that the members of each church can communicate, the priests celebrate and preach, in the churches of the other country. An agreement of inter-communion could only lead toward reunion in one of two events: the unlikely event of a political union of the two nations, or the ultimate event of a world-wide reunion of Christians. Reunion, on the other hand, means in effect either reunion of one or another body having episcopal government, with the Church of Rome, or reunion between bodies separated from each other in the same areas. The movements towards reunion which are at the present time most active, are of the second kind: reunion between the Anglican Church and one or more of the "Free Church" bodies. It is with the cultural implications of this latter kind of reunion that we are here specially concerned. There can be no question of reunion between the Church of England and, let us say, the Presbyterians or Methodists in America: any reunion would be of American Presbyterians with the Episcopal Church in America, and of English Presbyterians with the Church of England.

It should be obvious, from the considerations advanced in my first chapter, that complete reunion involves community of culture—some common culture already existing, and the potentiality of its further development consequent upon official reunion. The ideal reunion of all Christians does not, of course, imply an eventual *uniform* culture the world over: it implies simply a "Christian culture" of which all local cultures should be variants—and they would and should vary very widely indeed. We can already distinguish between a "local culture" and a "European culture"; when we use the latter term we recognise the local differences; similarly a universal "Christian culture" should not be taken to ignore or override the differences between the cultures of the several continents. But the existence of a strong community of culture between various Christian bodies in the same area (we must remember that we here mean "culture" as distinguished from "religion") not only facilitates reunion of Christians in that area, but exposes such reunion to peculiar dangers.

I have put forward the view that every division of a Christian people into sects brings about or aggravates the development of "sub-cultures" amongst that people; and I have asked the reader to examine Anglicanism and the Free Churches for confirmation of this view. But it should now be added, that the cultural divisions between Anglicans and Free Churchmen have, under changing social and economic conditions, become attenuated. The organisation of rural society from which the Church of England drew much of its cultural strength is in decay; the landed gentry have less security, less power and less influence; the families which have risen in trade and in many places succeeded to territorial proprietorship are themselves progressively reduced and impoverished. A diminishing number of Anglican clergy come from public schools or the old universities, or are educated at their families' expense; bishops are not wealthy men, and are embarrassed in keeping up palaces. Anglican and Free Church laymen have been educated at the same universities and often at the same schools. And finally, they are all exposed to the same environment of a culture severed from religion. When men of different religious persuasions are drawn together by common interests and common anxieties, by their awareness of an increasingly oppressive non-Christian world, and by their unawareness of the extent to which they are themselves penetrated by non-Christian influences and by a neutral culture, it is only to be expected that the vestiges of the distinctions between their several Christian cultures should seem to them of minor significance.

With the dangers of reunion on erroneous or evasive terms I am not here concerned; but I am much concerned with the danger that reunion facilitated by the disappearance of the cultural characteristics of the several bodies reunited might accelerate and confirm the general lowering of culture. The refinement or crudity of theological and philosophical thinking is itself, of course, one of the measures of the state of our culture; and the tendency in some quarters to reduce theology to such principles as a child can understand or a Socinian accept, is itself indicative of cultural debility. But there is a further danger, from our point of view, in schemes of reunion which attempt to remove the difficulties, and protect the self-assertiveness, of everybody. In an age like our own, when it has become a point of politeness to dissimulate social distinctions, and to pretend that the highest degree of "culture" ought to be made accessible to everybody—in an age of cultural levelling, it will be denied that the several Christian fragments to be re-united represent any cultural differences. There is certain to be a strong pressure towards a reunion on terms of complete cultural equality. Too much account may even be taken of the relative numbers of the membership of the uniting bodies: for a main culture will remain a main culture, and a sub-culture will remain a sub-culture, even if the latter attracts more adherents than the former. It is always the main religious body which is the guardian of more of the remains of the higher developments of culture preserved from a past time before the division took place. Not only is it the main religious body which has the more elaborated theology; it is the main religious body which is the least alienated from the best intellectual and artistic activity of its time. Hence it is that the convert—and I think not only of conversion from one form of Christianity to another, but indeed primarily of conversion from indifference to Christian belief and practice—the convert of the intellectual or sensitive type is drawn towards the more Catholic type of worship and doctrine. This attraction, which may occur before the prospective convert has begun to inform himself about Christianity at all, may be cited by the outsider as evidence that the convert has become a Christian for the wrong reasons, or that he is guilty of insincerity and affectation. Every sin that can be imagined has been practised, and the pretence of religious faith may often enough have cloaked intellectual or esthetic vanity and self-indulgence; but, on the view of the intimacy of religion and culture which is the starting point of my examination, such phenomena as the progress to religious faith through cultural attraction are both natural and acceptable.

Unity and Diversity: Sect and Cult

After the considerations now reviewed, I must attempt to link the chapter to the two preceding chapters, by enquiring what is the ideal pattern of unity and diversity between Christian nations and between the several strata in each nation. It should be obvious that the sociological point of view cannot lead us to those conclusions which can properly be reached only by theological premisses; and the reader of the previous chapters will be prepared to find no solution in any rigid and unchangeable scheme. No security against cultural deterioration is offered by any of the three chief types of religious organisation: the international church with a central government, the national church, or the separated sect. The danger of freedom is deliquescence; the danger of strict order is petrifaction. Nor can we judge from the history of any particular society, whether a different religious history would have resulted in a more healthy culture today. The disastrous effects of armed religious strife within a people, as in England in the seventeenth century or in the German States in the sixteenth, need no emphasis; the disintegrating effect of sectarian division has already been touched upon. Yet we may ask whether Methodism did not, in the period of its greatest fervour, revive the spiritual life of the English, and prepare the way for the Evangelical Movement and even for the Oxford Movement. Furthermore, Dissent made it possible for "working class" Christians (though perhaps it might have done more than it has for "labouring class" Christians) to play that part, which all zealous and socially active Christians should wish to play, in the conduct of their local church and the social and charitable organisations connected with it.[1] The actual choice, at times, has been between sectarianism and indifference; and those who chose the former were, in so doing, keeping alive the culture of certain social strata. And,

[1] See two valuable Supplements to *The Christian News-Letter:* "Ecumenical Christianity and the Working Classes" by W. G. Symons, July 30, 1941; and "The Free Churches and Working Class Culture" by John Marsh, May 20, 1942.

as I have said at the beginning, the appropriate culture of each stratum is of equal importance.

As in the relation between the social classes, and as in the relation of the several regions of a country to each other and to the central power, it would seem that a constant struggle between the centripetal and the centrifugal forces is desirable. For without the struggle no balance can be maintained; and if either force won the result would be deplorable. The conclusions to which we are justified in coming, from our premises and from the sociologist's point of view, appear to me to be as follows. Christendom should be one: the form of organisation and the locus of powers in that unity are questions upon which we cannot pronounce. But within that unity there should be an endless conflict between ideas—for it is only by the struggle against constantly appearing false ideas that the truth is enlarged and clarified, and in the conflict with heresy that orthodoxy is developed to meet the needs of the times; an endless effort also on the part of each region to shape its Christianity to suit itself, an effort which should neither be wholly suppressed nor left wholly unchecked. The local temperament must express its particularity in its form of Christianity, and so must the social stratum, so that the culture proper to each area and each class may flourish; but there must also be a force holding these areas and these classes together. If this corrective force in the direction of uniformity of belief and practice is lacking, then the culture of each part will suffer. We have already found that the culture of a nation prospers with the prosperity of the culture of its several constituents, both geographical and social; but that it also needs to be itself a part of a larger culture, which requires the ultimate ideal, however unrealisable, of a "world culture" in a sense different from that implicit in the schemes of world-federationists. And without a common faith, all efforts towards drawing nations closer together in culture can produce only an illusion of unity.

CHAPTER V

A Note on Culture and Politics

Politics did not, however, so much engage him as to withhold his thoughts from things of more importance.

SAMUEL JOHNSON on GEORGE LYTTELTON

W E observe nowadays that "culture" attracts the attention of men of politics: not that politicians are always "men of culture," but that "culture" is recognised both as an instrument of policy and as something socially desirable which it is the business of the State to promote. We not only hear, from high political quarters, that "cultural relations" between nations are of great importance, but find that bureaux are founded, and officials appointed, for the express purpose of attending to these relations, which are presumed to foster international amity. The fact that culture has become, in some sense, a department of politics, should not obscure in our memory the fact that at other periods politics has been an activity pursued within a culture, and between representatives of different cultures. It is therefore not impertinent to attempt to indicate the place of politics within a culture united and divided according to the kind of unity and division which we have been considering.

We may assume, I think, that in a society so articulated the practice of politics and an active interest in public affairs

84

would not be the business of everybody, or of everybody to
the same degree; and that not everybody should concern
himself, except at moments of crisis, with the conduct of the
nation as a whole. In a healthily *regional* society, public affairs
would be the business of everybody, or of the great majority,
only within very small social units; and would be the business of a progressively smaller number of men in the larger
units within which the smaller were comprehended. In a
healthily *stratified* society, public affairs would be a responsibility not equally borne: a greater responsibility would
be inherited by those who inherited special advantages,
and in whom self-interest, and interest for the sake of
their families ("a stake in the country") should cohere
with public spirit. The governing élite, of the nation as a
whole, would consist of those whose responsibility was inherited with their affluence and position, and whose forces
were constantly increased, and often led, by rising individuals
of exceptional talents. But when we speak of a governing élite,
we must safeguard ourselves against thinking of an élite
sharply divided from the other élites of society.

The relation of the political élite—by which we mean the
leading members of *all* the effective and recognised political
groups: for the survival of a parliamentary system requires
a constant *dining with the Opposition*[1]—to the other élites
would be put too crudely if described as communication between men of action and men of thought. It is rather a
relation between men of different types of mind and different areas of thought and action. A sharp distinction between
thought and action is no more tenable for the political than
for the religious life, in which the contemplative must have
his own activity, and the secular priest must not be wholly
unpractised in meditation. There is no plane of active life
on which thought is negligible, except that of the merest

[1] I seem to remember that some such phrase was either attributed
to Sir William Vernon Harcourt, or used about him.

automatic execution of orders; and there is no species of thinking which can be quite without effect upon action.

I have suggested elsewhere [1] that a society is in danger of disintegration when there is a lack of contact between people of different areas of activity—between the political, the scientific, the artistic, the philosophical and the religious minds. This separation cannot be repaired merely by public organisation. It is not a question of assembling into committees representatives of different types of knowledge and experience, of calling in everybody to advise everybody else. The élite should be something different, something much more organically composed, than a panel of bonzes, caciques and tycoons. Men who meet only for definite serious purposes, and on official occasions, do not wholly meet. They may have some common concern very much at heart; they may, in the course of repeated contacts, come to share a vocabulary and an idiom which appear to communicate every shade of meaning necessary for their common purpose; but they will continue to retire from these encounters each to his private social world as well as to his solitary world. Everyone has observed that the possibilities of contented silence, of a mutual happy awareness when engaged upon a common task, or an underlying seriousness and significance in the enjoyment of a silly joke, are characteristics of any close personal intimacy; and the congeniality of any circle of friends depends upon a common social convention, a common ritual, and common pleasures of relaxation. These aids to intimacy are no less important for the communication of meaning in words, than the possession of a common subject upon which the several parties are informed. It is unfortunate for a man when his friends and his business associates are two unrelated groups; it is also narrowing when they are one and the same group.

Such observations upon personal intimacy cannot pretend

[1] *The Idea of a Christian Society,* p. 40.

to any novelty: the only possible novelty is in calling attention to them in this context. They point to the desirability of
a society in which persons of every superior activity can meet
without merely talking shop or being at pains to talk each
other's shop. In order correctly to appraise a man of action
we must meet him: or we must at least have known enough
men of similar pursuits to be able to draw a shrewd guess
about one whom we have not met. And to meet a man of
thought, and to form an impression of his personality, may be
of great assistance in judging his ideas. This is not wholly
improper even in the field of art, though with important
reservations, and though the impressions of an artist's personality often affect opinion of his work quite irrelevantly—for
every artist must have remarked, that while a small number
of people dislike his work more strongly after meeting him,
there are also many who are more friendly disposed towards
his work if they find him a pleasant fellow. These advantages
persist however they may offend the reason, and in spite of the
fact that in modern societies of large numbers, it is impossible
for everyone to know everyone else.

In our time, we read too many new books, or are oppressed
by the thought of the new books which we are neglecting to
read; we read many books, because we cannot know enough
people; we cannot know everybody whom it would be to our
benefit to know, because there are too many of them. Consequently, if we have the skill to put words together and the
fortune to get them printed, we communicate by writing more
books. It is often those writers whom we are lucky enough to
know, whose books we can ignore; and the better we know
them personally, the less need we may feel to read what they
write. We are encumbered not only with too many new books:
we are further embarrassed by too many periodicals, reports
and privately circulated memoranda. In the endeavour to
keep up with the most intelligent of these publications we
may sacrifice the three permanent reasons for reading: the

acquisition of wisdom, the enjoyment of art, and the pleasure of entertainment. Meanwhile, the professional politician has too much to do to have leisure for serious reading, even on politics. He has far too little time for exchange of ideas and information with men of distinction in other walks of life. In a society of smaller size (a society, therefore, which was less feverishly *busy*) there might be more conversation and fewer books; and we should not find the tendency—of which this essay provides one example—for those who have acquired some reputation, to write books outside the subject on which they have made that reputation.

It is unlikely, in all the mass of letterpress, that the profoundest and most original works will reach the eye or command the attention of a large public, or even of a good number of the readers who are qualified to appreciate them. The ideas which flatter a current tendency or emotional attitude will go farthest; and some others will be distorted to fit in with what is already accepted. The residuum in the public mind is hardly likely to be a distillation of the best and wisest: it is more likely to represent the common prejudices of the majority of editors and reviewers. In this way are formed the *idées reçues*—more precisely the *mots reçus* —which, because of their emotional influence upon that part of the public which is influenced by printed matter, have to be taken into account by the professional politician, and treated with respect in his public utterances. It is unnecessary, for the simultaneous reception of these "ideas," that they should be consistent among themselves; and, however they contradict each other, the practical politician must handle them with as much deference as if they were the constructions of informed sagacity, the intuitions of genius, or the accumulated wisdom of ages. He has not, as a rule, inhaled any fragrance they may have had when they were fresh; he only noses them when they have already begun to stink.

In a society so graded as to have several levels of culture, and several levels of power and authority, the politician might at least be restrained, in his use of language, by his respect for the judgment, and fear of the ridicule, of a smaller and more critical public, among which was maintained some standard of prose style. If it were also a decentralised society, a society in which local cultures continued to flourish, and in which the majority of problems were local problems on which local populations could form an opinion from their own experience and from conversation with their neighbours, political utterances might also tend to manifest greater clarity and be susceptible of fewer variations of interpretation. A local speech on a local issue is likely to be more intelligible than one addressed to a whole nation, and we observe that the greatest muster of ambiguities and obscure generalities is usually to be found in speeches which are addressed to the whole world.

It is always desirable that a part of the education of those persons who are either born into, or qualified by their abilities to enter, the superior political grades of society, should be instruction in history, and that a part of the study of history should be the history of political theory. The advantage of the study of Greek history and Greek political theory, as a preliminary to the study of other history and other theory, is its *manageability:* it has to do with a small area, with men rather than masses, and with the human passions of individuals rather than with those vast impersonal forces which in our modern society are a necessary convenience of thought, and the study of which tends to obscure the study of human beings. The reader of Greek philosophy, moreover, is unlikely to be over-sanguine about the effects of political theory; for he will observe that the study of political forms appears to have arisen out of the failure of political systems; and that neither Plato nor Aristotle was much concerned with prediction, or very optimistic about the future.

A Note on Culture and Politics

The kind of political theory which has arisen in quite modern times is less concerned with human nature, which it is inclined to treat as something which can always be re-fashioned to fit whatever political form is regarded as most desirable. Its real data are impersonal forces which may have originated in the conflict and combination of human wills but have come to supersede them. As a part of academic discipline for the young, it suffers from several drawbacks. It tends, of course, to form minds which will be set to think only in terms of impersonal and inhuman forces, and thereby to de-humanise its students. Being occupied with humanity only in the mass, it tends to separate itself from ethics; being occupied only with that recent period of history during which humanity can most easily be shown to have been ruled by impersonal forces, it reduces the proper study of mankind to the last two or three hundred years of man. It too often inculcates a belief in a future inflexibly determined and at the same time in a future which we are wholly free to shape as we like. Modern political thought, inextricably involved with economics and with sociology, preempts to itself the position of queen of the sciences. For the exact and experimental sciences are judged according to their utility, and are valued in so far as they produce results—either for making life more comfortable and less laborious, or for making it more precarious and ending it more quickly. Culture itself is regarded either as a negligible by-product which can be left to itself, or as a department of life to be organised in accordance with the particular scheme we favour. I am thinking not only of the more dogmatic and totalitarian philosophies of the present day, but of assumptions which colour thinking in every country and tend to be shared by the most opposed parties.

An important document in the history of the political direction of culture will be Leon Trotsky's essay, *Literature and Revolution,* of which an English translation appeared in

A Note on Culture and Politics

1925.[1] The conviction, which seems to be deeply implanted in the Muscovite mind, that it is the role of Mother Russia to contribute not merely ideas and political forms, but a total way of life for the rest of the world, has gone far to make us all more politically culture-conscious. But there have been other causes than the Russian Revolution for this consciousness. The researches and the theories of anthropologists have played their part, and have led us to study the relations of imperial powers and subject peoples with a new attention. Governments are more aware of the necessity of taking account of cultural differences; and to the degree to which colonial administration is controlled from the imperial centre, these differences become of increasing importance. One people in isolation is not aware of having a "culture" at all. And the differences between the several European nations in the past were not wide enough to make their peoples see their cultures as different to the point of conflict and incompatibility: culture-consciousness as a means of uniting a nation against other nations was first exploited by the late rulers of Germany. Today, we have become culture-conscious in a way which nourishes nazism, communism and nationalism all at once; in a way which emphasises separation without helping us to overcome it. At this point a few remarks on the cultural effects of empire (in the most comprehensive sense) may not be amiss.

The early British rulers of India were content to rule; some of them, through long residence and continuous absence from Britain, assimilated themselves to the mentality of the

[1] Published by International Publishers, New York. A book which merits republication. It does not give the impression that Trotsky was very sensitive to literature; but he was, from his own point of view, very intelligent about it. Like all his writings, the book is encumbered with discussion of minor Russian personalities of which the foreigner is ignorant and in which he is not interested; but this indulgence in detail, while it contributes a flavour of provinciality, gives the work all the more appearance of genuineness, as having been written rather to speak his mind than with an eye to a foreign audience.

people they governed. A later type of rulers, explicitly and increasingly the servants of Whitehall, and serving only for a limited period (after which they returned to their native country, either to retirement or to some other activity) aimed rather to bring to India the benefits of western civilisation. They did not intend to uproot, or to impose, a total "culture": but the superiority of western political and social organisation, of English education, of English justice, of western "enlightenment" and science seemed to them so self-evident that the desire to do good would alone have been a sufficient motive for introducing these things. The Briton, unconscious of the importance of religion in the formation of his own culture, could hardly be expected to recognise its importance in the preservation of another. In the piece-meal imposition of a foreign culture—an imposition in which force plays only a small part: the appeal to ambition, and the temptation to which the native is exposed, to admire the wrong things in western civilisation, and for the wrong reasons, are much more decisive—the motives of arrogance and generosity are always inextricably mixed; there is at the same time an assertion of superiority and a desire to communicate the way of life upon which that assumed superiority is based; so that the native acquires a taste for western ways, a jealous admiration of material power, and a resentment against his tutors. The partial success of westernisation, of which some members of an Eastern society are quick to seize the apparent advantages, has tended to make the Oriental more discontented with his own civilisation and more resentful of that which has caused this discontent; has made him more conscious of differences, at the same time that it has obliterated some of these differences; and has broken up the native culture on its highest level, without penetrating the mass. And we are left with the melancholy reflection that the cause of this disintegration is not corruption, brutality or maladministration: such ills have played but a small part, and no ruling nation has had less to be ashamed of than Britain in these particulars; corruption, brutality and maladministration were too prevalent in India before the British arrived, for commission of them to disturb the fabric of Indian life. The cause lies in the fact that there can be no permanent compromise between the extremes of an external rule which is content to keep order and leave the social structure unaltered, and a complete cultural assimilation. The failure to arrive at the latter is a religious failure.[1]

To point to the damage that has been done to native cultures in the process of imperial expansion is by no means an indictment of empire itself, as the advocates of imperial dissolution are only too apt to infer. Indeed, it is often these same anti-imperialists who, being liberals, are the most complacent believers in the superiority of western civilisation, and at one and the same time blind to the benefits conferred by imperial government and to the injury done by the destruction of native culture. According to such enthusiasts, we do well to intrude ourselves upon another civilisation, equip the members of it with our mechanical contrivances, our systems of government, education, law, medicine and finance, inspire them with a contempt for their own customs and with an enlightened attitude towards religious superstition—and then leave them to stew in the broth which we have brewed for them.

[1] An interesting survey of the effects of culture-contact in the East is to be found in *The British in Asia* by Guy Wint. Mr. Wint's occasional suggestions of the effect of India upon the British are no less suggestive than his account of the effect of the British upon India. For example:

"How the English colour prejudice began—whether it was inherited from the Portuguese in India, or was an infection from the Hindu caste system or, as has been suggested, began with the arrival of insular and suburban wives of civil servants, or came from some other cause—is not certain. The British in India were the British middle class living in the artificial condition of having above them no upper class of their own people, and below them no lower class of their own people. It was a state of existence which led to a combined arrogance and defensiveness." P. 209.

A Note on Culture and Politics

It is noticeable that the most vehement criticism, or abuse, of British imperialism often comes from representatives of societies which practise a different form of imperialism—that is to say, of expansion which brings material benefits and extends the influence of culture. America has tended to impose its way of life chiefly in the course of doing business, and creating a taste for its commodities. Even the humblest material artefact, which is the product and the symbol of a particular civilisation, is an emissary of the culture out of which it comes: I mention that influential and inflammable article the celluloid film. American economic expansion can be also, in its way, the cause of disintegration of cultures which it touches.

The newest type of imperialism, that of Russia, is probably the most ingenious, and the best calculated to flourish according to the temper of the present age. The Russian Empire appears to be sedulous to avoid the weaknesses of the empires which have preceded it: it is at the same time more ruthless and more careful of the vanity of subject peoples. The official doctrine is one of complete racial equality—an appearance easier for Russia to preserve in Asia, because of the oriental cast of the Russian mind and because of the backwardness of Russian development according to western standards. Attempts appear to be made to preserve the similitude of local self-government and autonomy: the aim, I suspect, is to give the several local republics and satellite states the illusion of a kind of independence, while the real power is exercised from Moscow. The illusion must sometimes fade, when a local republic is suddenly and ignominiously reduced to the status of a kind of province or crown colony; but it is maintained—and this is what is most interesting from our point of view—by a careful fostering of local "culture," culture in the reduced sense of the word, as everything that is picturesque, harmless and separable from politics, such as language and literature, local arts and customs. But as Soviet Russia must

94

maintain the subordination of culture to political theory, the success of her imperialism seems likely to lead to a sense of superiority on the part of that one of her peoples in which her political theory has been formed; so that we might expect, so long as the Russian Empire holds together, to find the increasing assertion of one dominant Muscovite culture, with subordinate races surviving, not as peoples each with its own cultural pattern, but as inferior castes. However that may be, the Russians have been the first modern people to practise the political direction of culture consciously, and to attack at every point the culture of any people whom they wish to dominate. The more highly developed is any alien culture, the more thorough the attempts to extirpate it by elimination of those elements in the subject population in which that culture is most conscious.

The dangers arising from "culture-consciousness" in the West are at present of a different kind. Our motives, in attempting to do something about our culture, are not yet consciously political. They arise from the consciousness that our culture is not in very good health and from the feeling that we must take steps to improve its condition. This consciousness has transformed the problem of education, by either identifying culture with education, or turning to education as the one instrument for improving our culture. As for the intervention of the State, or of some quasi-official body subventioned by the State, in assistance of the arts and sciences, we can see only too well the need, under present conditions, for such support. A body like the British Council, by constantly sending representatives of the arts and sciences abroad, and inviting foreign representatives to this country, is in our time invaluable—but we must not come to accept as permanent or normal and healthy the conditions which make such direction necessary. We are prepared to believe that there will, under any conditions, be useful work for the British Council to perform; but we should not like to be assured that

95

never again will it be possible for the intellectual élite of all
countries to travel as private citizens and make each other's
acquaintance without the approval and support of some official organisation. Some important activities, it is likely
enough, will never again be possible without official backing
of some kind. The progress of the experimental sciences now
requires vast and expensive equipment; and the practice of
the arts has no longer, on any large scale, the benefit of private
patronage. Some safeguard may be provided, against increasing centralisation of control and politicisation of the arts and
sciences, by encouraging local initiative and responsibility;
and, as far as possible, separating the central source of funds
from control over their use. We should do well also to refer
to the subsidised and artificially stimulated activities each by
its name: let us do what is necessary for painting and sculp-
ture, or architecture, or the theatre, or music, or one or another science or department of intellectual exercise, speaking
of each by its name, and restraining ourselves from using the
word "culture" as a comprehensive term. For thus we slip into
the assumption that culture can be planned. Culture can never
be wholly conscious—there is always more to it than we are
conscious of; and it cannot be planned because it is also the
unconscious background of all our planning.

CHAPTER VI

Notes on Education and Culture: and Conclusion

D URING the recent war an exceptional number of books were published on the subject of education; there were also voluminous reports of commissions, and an incalculable number of contributions on this subject in periodicals. It is not my business, nor is it within my competence, to review the whole of current educational theory; but a few comments on it are in place, because of the close association, in many minds, between education and culture. What is of interest to my thesis is the kind of assumption which is made by those who write about education. The notes which follow comment on a few such prevalent assumptions.

1. *That, before entering upon any discussion of Education, the purpose of Education must be stated.*

This is a very different thing from defining the word "education." The Oxford Dictionary tells us that education is "the process of bringing up (young persons)"; that it is "the systematic instruction, schooling or training given to the young (and, by extension, to adults) in preparation for the work of life"; that it is also "culture or development of powers, formation of character." We learn that the first of these definitions is according to the use of the sixteenth century; and that the third use appears to have arisen in the nineteenth. In short, the dictionary tells you what you know already, and I do not see how a dictionary could do more. But when writers attempt to state the *purpose* of education, they are doing one of two things: they are eliciting what they believe to have been the unconscious purpose always, and thereby giving their own meaning to the history of the subject; or they are formulating what may not have been, or may have been only fitfully, the real purpose in the past, but should in their opinion be the purpose directing development in the future. Let us look at a few of these statements of the purpose of education. In *The Churches Survey Their Task,* a volume published in connexion with the Oxford Conference on Church, Community and State in 1937, we find the following:

> Education is the process by which the community seeks to open its life to all the individuals within it and enable them to take their part in it. It attempts to pass on to them its culture, including the standards by which it would have them live. Where that culture is regarded as final, the attempt is made to impose it on younger minds. Where it is viewed as a stage in development, younger minds are trained both to receive it and to criticise and improve upon it.
>
> This culture is composed of various elements. It runs from rudimentary skill and knowledge up to the interpretation of the universe and of man by which the community lives . . .

The purpose of education, it seems, is to transmit culture: so culture (which has not been defined) is likely to be limited to what can be transmitted by education. While "education" is perhaps allowed to be more comprehensive than "the educational system," we must observe that the assumption that culture can be summed up as skills and interpretations controverts the more comprehensive view of culture which I have endeavoured to take. Incidentally, we should keep a sharp eye on this personified "community" which is the repository of authority.

Another account of the purpose of education is that which sees it in terms of political and social change. This, if I have understood him, is the purpose which fires Mr. H. C. Dent. "Our ideal," he says in *A New Order in English Education,* "is a full democracy." Full democracy is not defined; and, if full democracy is attained, we should like to know what is to be our next ideal for education after this ideal has been realised.

Mr. Herbert Read gives his account of the purpose of education in *Education Through Art.* I do not think that Mr. Read could see quite eye to eye with Mr. Dent, for whereas Mr. Dent wants a "full democracy," Mr. Read says that he "elects for a libertarian conception of democracy," which I suspect is a very different democracy from Mr. Dent's. Mr. Read (in spite of *elects for*) is a good deal more precise in his use of words than Mr. Dent; so, while he is less likely to confuse the hasty reader, he is more likely to confound the diligent one. It is in electing for a libertarian conception of democracy, he says, that we answer the question, "What is the purpose of education?" This purpose is further defined as "the reconciliation of individual uniqueness with social unity."

Another kind of account of the purpose of education is the uncompleted account, of which Dr. F. C. Happold (in *Towards a New Aristocracy*) gives us a specimen. The fundamental task of education, he tells us, is "training the sort of men and women the age needs." If we believe that there are some sorts of men and women which are needed by every age, we may remark that there should be permanence as well as change in education. But the account is incomplete, in that we are left wondering who is to determine what are the needs of the age.

One of the most frequent answers to the question "what is the purpose of education?" is "happiness." Mr. Herbert Read gives us this answer too, in a pamphlet called *The Education of Free Men,* by saying that he knows of no better definition of the aims of education than that of William Godwin: "the true object of education . . . is the generation of happiness." "The Government's purpose," said the White Paper which heralded the latest Education Act, "is to secure for children a happier childhood and a better start in life." Happiness is often associated with "the full development of personality."

Dr. C. E. M. Joad, showing more prudence than most of those who attempt to answer this question, holds the view, which seems to me a very sensible one, that education has a number of ends. Of these he lists three (in *About Education,* one of the most readable books on the subject that I have consulted):

1. To enable a boy or girl to earn his or her living. . . .
2. To equip him to play his part as the citizen of a democracy.
3. To enable him to develop all the latent powers and faculties of his nature and so enjoy a good life.

It is a relief, at this point, to have presented to us the simple and intelligible notion that equipment to earn one's living is one of the purposes of education. We again note the close association between education and democracy; here also Dr. Joad is perhaps more prudent than Mr. Dent or Mr. Read in not qualifying his "democracy" by an adjective. "To develop all the latent powers and faculties" appears to be a variant of "the full development of personality": but Dr. Joad is sagacious in avoiding the use of that puzzling word "personality."

Some, no doubt, will disagree with Dr. Joad's selection of purposes. And we may, with more reason, complain that none of them takes us very far without getting us into trouble. They all contain some truth: but as each of them needs to be corrected by the others, it is possible that they all need to be adjusted to other purposes as well. Each of them needs some qualification. A particular course of education may, in the world in which a young person finds himself, be exactly what is needed to develop his peculiar gifts and yet impair his ability to earn a living. Education of the young to play their part in a democracy is a necessary adaptation of individual to environment, if a democracy is what they are going to play their part in: if not, it is making the pupil instrumental to the accomplishment of a social change which the educator has at heart—and this is not education but something else. I am not denying that a democracy is the best form of society, but by introducing this standard for education, Dr. Joad, with other writers, is leaving it open to those who believe in some other form of society which Dr. Joad might not like, to substitute (and so far as he is talking about education only, Dr. Joad could not confute them) some account like the following: "One of the purposes of education is to equip a boy or girl to play his or her part as the subject of a despotic government." Finally, as for developing all the latent powers and faculties of one's nature, I am not sure that anyone should hope for that: it may be that we can only develop some powers and faculties at the expense of others, and that there must be some choice, as well as inevitably some accident, in the direction which anyone's development takes. And as for the good life, there is some ambiguity in the sense in which we shall "enjoy" it; and what the good life is, has been a subject of discussion from early times to the present day.

What we remark especially about the educational thought of the last few years, is the enthusiasm with which education has been taken up as an instrument for the realisation of social ideals. It would be a pity if we overlooked the possibilities of education as a means of acquiring *wisdom;* if we belittled the acquisition of *knowledge* for the satisfaction of curiosity, without any further motive than the desire to know; and if we lost our respect for *learning.* So much for the purpose of education. I proceed to the next assumption.

2. *That Education makes people happier.*

We have already found that the purpose of education has been defined as the making people happier. The assumption that it *does* make people happier needs to be considered separately. That the educated person is happier than the uneducated is by no means self-evident. Those who are conscious of their lack of education are discontented, if they cherish ambitions to excel in occupations for which they are not qualified; they are sometimes discontented, simply because they have been given to understand that more education would have made them happier. Many of us feel some grievance against our elders, our schools or our universities for not having done better by us: this can be a way of extenuating our own shortcomings and excusing our failures. On the other hand, to be educated above the level of those whose social habits and tastes one has inherited, may cause a division within a man which interferes with happiness; even though, when the individual is of superior intellect, it may bring him a fuller and more useful life. And to be trained, taught or instructed above the level of one's abilities and strength may be disastrous; for education is a strain, and can impose greater burdens upon a mind than that mind can bear. Too much education, like too little education, can produce unhappiness.

3. *That Education is something that everyone wants.*

People can be persuaded to desire almost anything, for a time, if they are constantly told that it is something to which they are entitled and which is unjustly withheld from them. The spontaneous desire for education is greater in some communities than in others; it is generally agreed to be stronger in the North than in the South of England, and stronger still in Scotland. It is possible that the desire for education is greater where there are difficulties in the way of obtaining it—difficulties not insuperable but only to be surmounted at the cost of some sacrifice and privation. If this is so, we may conjecture that facility of education will lead to indifference to it; and that the universal imposition of education up to the years of maturity will lead to hostility towards it. A high average of general education is perhaps less necessary for a civil society than is a respect for learning.

4. *That Education should be organised so as to give "equality of opportunity."* [1]

It follows from what has been said in an earlier chapter about classes and élites, that education should help to preserve the class and to select the élite. It is right that the exceptional individual should have the opportunity to elevate himself in the social scale and attain a position in which he can exercise his talents to the greatest benefit of himself and of society. But the ideal of an educational system which would automatically sort out everyone according to his native capacities is unattainable in practice; and if we made it our chief aim, would disorganise society and debase education. It would disorganise society, by substituting for classes, élites of brains, or perhaps only of sharp wits. Any educational system aiming at a complete adjustment between education and society will tend both to restrict education to what will lead to success in the world, and to restrict success in the world to those persons who have been good pupils of the system. The pros-

[1] This may be called Jacobinism in Education. Jacobinism, according to one who had given some attention to it, consisted "in taking the people as equal individuals, without any corporate name or description, without attention to property, without division of powers, and forming the government of delegates from a number of men, so constituted; in destroying or confiscating property, and bribing the public creditors, or the poor, with the spoils, now of one part of the community, now of another, without regard to prescription or profession."—Burke: *Remarks on the Policy of the Allies.*

pect of a society ruled and directed only by those who have passed certain examinations or satisfied tests devised by psychologists is not reassuring: while it might give scope to talents hitherto obscured, it would probably obscure others, and reduce to impotence some who should have rendered high service. Furthermore, the ideal of a uniform system such that no one capable of receiving higher education could fail to get it, leads imperceptibly to the education of too many people, and consequently to the lowering of standards to whatever this swollen number of candidates is able to reach.

Nothing is more moving in Dr. Joad's treatise than the passage in which he expatiates on the amenities of Winchester and Oxford. Dr. Joad paid a visit to Winchester; and while there, he wandered into a delightful garden. One suspects that he may have got into the garden of the Deanery, but he does not know what garden it was. This garden set him to ruminating about the College, and its "blend of the works of nature and man." "What I see," he said to himself, "is the end-product of a long-continuing tradition, running back through our history, in this particular case, to the Tudors." (I cannot see why he stopped at the Tudors, but that was far enough to sustain the emotion with which his mind was suffused.) It was not only nature and architecture that impressed him; he was aware also of "a long tradition of secure men leading dignified and leisured lives." From Winchester his mind passed to Oxford, to the Oxford which he had known as an undergraduate; and again, it was not merely architecture and gardens upon which his mind dwelt, but also men:

But even in my own time . . . when democracy was already knocking at the gates of the citadel it was so soon to capture, some faint aftermath of the Greek sunset could be observed. At Balliol, in 1911 there was a group of young men centring upon the Grenfells and John Manners, many of whom were killed in the last war, who took it for granted that they should row in the College boat, play hockey or rugger for the College or even for the University, act for the O.U.D.S., get tight at College Gaudies, spend part of the night talking in the company of their friends, while at the same time getting their scholarships and prizes and Firsts in Greats. The First in Greats was taken, as it were, in their stride. I have not seen such men before or since. It may be that they were the last representatives of a tradition which died with them. . . .

It seems strange, after these wistful reflections, that Dr. Joad should end his chapter by supporting a proposal of Mr. R. H. Tawney: that the public schools should be taken over by the State and used as boarding schools to accommodate for two or three years the intellectually abler secondary school boys from the ages of sixteen to eighteen. For the conditions over which he pronounces such a tearful valedictory were not brought about by equality of opportunity. They were not brought about, either, by mere privilege; but by a happy combination of privilege and opportunity, in the *blend* he so savours, of which no Education Act will ever find the secret.

5. *The Mute Inglorious Milton dogma.*

The Equality of Opportunity dogma, which is associated with the belief that superiority is always superiority of intellect, that some infallible method can be designed for the detection of intellect, and that a system can be devised which will infallibly nourish it, derives emotional reinforcement from the belief in the mute inglorious Milton. This myth assumes that a great deal of first-rate ability—not merely ability, but genius—is being wasted for lack of education; or, alternatively, that if even one potential Milton has been suppressed in the course of centuries, from deprivation of formal teaching, it is still worth while to turn education topsy-turvy so that it may not happen again. (It might be embarrassing to have a great many Miltons and Shakespeares, but that danger is remote.) In justice to Thomas Gray, we should remind ourselves of the last and finest line of the quatrain, and remember that we may also have escaped some Cromwell *guilty* of his country's blood. The proposition that we have lost a number of Miltons and Cromwells through our tardiness in providing a comprehensive state system of education, cannot be either proved or disproved: it has a strong attraction for many ardent reforming spirits.

This completes my brief list—which is not intended to be exhaustive—of current beliefs. The dogma of equal opportunity is the most influential of all, and is maintained stoutly by some who would shrink from what seem to me its probable consequences. It is an ideal which can only be fully realised when the institution of the family is no longer respected, and when parental control and responsibility passes to the State. Any system which puts it into effect must see that no advantages of family fortune, no advantages due to the foresight, the self-sacrifice or the ambition of parents are allowed to obtain for any child or young person an education superior to that to which the system finds him to be entitled. The popularity of the belief is perhaps an indication that the depression of the family is accepted, and that the disintegration of classes is far advanced. This disintegration of classes had already led to an exaggerated estimate of the social importance of the right school and the right college at the right university, as giving a status which formerly pertained to mere birth. In a more articulated society—which is *not* a society in which social classes are isolated from each other: that is itself a kind of decay—the social distinction of the right school or college would not be so coveted, for social position would be marked in other ways. The envy of those who are "better born" than oneself is a feeble velleity, with only a shadow of the passion with which material advantages are envied. No sane person can be consumed with bitterness at not having had more exalted ancestors, for that would be to wish to be another person than the person one is: but the advantage of the status conferred by education at a more fashionable school is one which we can readily imagine ourselves as having enjoyed also. The disintegration of class has induced the expansion of envy, which provides ample fuel for the flame of "equal opportunity."

Besides the motive of giving everyone as much education as possible, because education is in itself desirable, there are other motives affecting educational legislation: motives which may be praiseworthy, or which simply recognise the inevitable, and which we need mention here only as a reminder of the complexity of the legislative problem. One motive, for instance, for raising the age-limit of compulsory schooling is the laudable desire to protect the adolescent, and fortify him against the more degrading influences to which he is exposed on entering the ranks of industry. We should be candid about such a motive; and instead of affirming what is to be doubted, that everyone will profit by as many years of tuition as we can give him, admit that the conditions of life in modern industrial society are so deplorable, and the moral restraints so weak, that we must prolong the schooling of young people simply because we are at our wits' end to know what to do to save them. Instead of congratulating ourselves on our progress, whenever the school assumes another responsibility hitherto left to parents, we might do better to admit that we have arrived at a stage of civilisation at which the family is irresponsible, or incompetent, or helpless; at which parents cannot be expected to train their children properly; at which many parents cannot afford to feed them properly, and would not know how, even if they had the means; and that Education must step in and make the best of a bad job.[1]

[1] I hope, however, that the reader of these lines has read, or will immediately read, *The Peckham Experiment,* as an illustration of what can be done, under modern conditions, to help the family to help itself.

Notes on Education and Culture: and Conclusion

Mr. D. R. Hardman [1] observed that:

The age of industrialism and democracy had brought to an end most of the great cultural traditions of Europe, and not least that of architecture. In the contemporary world, in which the majority were half-educated and many not even a quarter-educated, and in which large fortunes and enormous power could be obtained by exploiting ignorance and appetite, there was a vast cultural breakdown which stretched from America to Europe and from Europe to the East.

This is true, though there are a few inferences which might be improperly drawn. The exploitation of ignorance and appetite is not an activity only of commercial adventurers making large fortunes: it can be pursued more thoroughly and on a larger scale by governments. The cultural breakdown is not a kind of infection which began in America, spread to Europe, and from Europe has contaminated the East (Mr. Hardman may not have meant that, but his words might be so interpreted). But what is important is to remember that "half-education" is a modern phenomenon. In earlier ages the majority could not be said to have been "half-educated" or less: people had the education necessary for the functions they were called upon to perform. It would be incorrect to refer to a member of a primitive society, or to a skilled agricultural labourer in any age, as half-educated or quarter-educated or educated to any smaller fraction. *Education* in the modern sense implies a disintegrated society, in which it has come to be assumed that there must be one measure of education according to which everyone is educated simply more or less. Hence *Education* has become an abstraction.

Once we have arrived at this abstraction, remote from life, it is easy to proceed to the conclusion—for we all agree about the "cultural breakdown"—that education for every-

[1] As Parliamentary Secretary to the Ministry of Education, speaking on January 12, 1946, at the general meeting of the Middlesex Head Teachers' Association.

body is the means we must employ for putting civilisation together again. Now so long as we mean by "education" everything that goes to form the good individual in a good society, we are in accord, though the conclusion does not appear to get us anywhere; but when we come to mean by "education" that limited system of instruction which the Ministry of Education controls, or aims to control, the remedy is manifestly and ludicrously inadequate. The same may be said of the definition of the purpose of education which we have already found in *The Churches Survey Their Task*. According to this definition, education is the process by which the community attempts to pass on to all its members its culture, including the standards by which it would have them live. The community, in this definition, is an unconscious collective mind, very different from the mind of the Ministry of Education, or the Head Masters' Association, or the mind of any of the numerous bodies concerned with education. If we include as education all the influences of family and environment, we are going far beyond what professional educators can control—though their sway can extend very far indeed; but if we mean that culture is what is passed on by our elementary and secondary schools, or by our preparatory and public schools, then we are asserting that an organ is a whole organism. For the schools can transmit only a part, and they can only transmit this part effectively, if the outside influences, not only of family and environment, but of work and play, of newsprint and spectacles and entertainment and sport, are in harmony with them.

Error creeps in again and again through our tendency to think of culture as group culture exclusively, the culture of the "cultured" classes and élites. We then proceed to think of the humbler part of society as having culture only in so far as it participates in this superior and more conscious culture. To treat the "uneducated" mass of the population as we might treat some innocent tribe of savages to whom we

are impelled to deliver the true faith, is to encourage them
to neglect or despise that culture which they should possess
and from which the more conscious part of culture draws
vitality; and to aim to make everyone share in the appreciation of the fruits of the more conscious part of culture is to
adulterate and cheapen what you give. For it is an essential
condition of the preservation of the quality of the culture of
the minority, that it should continue to be a minority culture.
No number of Young Peoples' Colleges will compensate for
the deterioration of Oxford and Cambridge, and for the disappearance of that "blend" which Dr. Joad relishes. A "mass-
culture" will always be a substitute-culture; and sooner or
later the deception will become apparent to the more intelligent of those upon whom this culture has been palmed off.

I am not questioning the usefulness, or deriding the dig-
nity of Young Peoples' Colleges, or of any other particular
new construction. In so far as these institutions can be good,
they are more likely to be good, and not to deliver disappoint-
ment, if we are frankly aware of the limits of what we can do
with them, and if we combat the delusion that the maladies of
the modern world can be put right by a system of instruction.
A measure which is desirable as a palliative, may be injurious
if presented as a cure. My main point is the same as that
which I tried to make in the previous chapter, when I spoke of
the tendency of politics to dominate culture, instead of keeping to its place within a culture. There is also the danger that
education—which indeed comes under the influence of politics
—will take upon itself the reformation and direction of culture, instead of keeping to its place as one of the activities
through which a culture realises itself. Culture cannot altogether be brought to consciousness; and the culture of which
we are wholly conscious is never the whole of culture: the
effective culture is that which is directing the activities of
those who are manipulating that which they *call* culture.

So the instructive point is this, that the more education

arrogates to itself the responsibility, the more systematically will it betray culture. The definition of the purpose of education in *The Churches Survey Their Task* returns to plague us like the laughter of hyaenas at a funeral. *Where that culture is regarded as final, the attempt is made to impose it on younger minds. Where it is viewed as a stage in development, younger minds are trained to receive it and to improve upon it.* These are cosseting phrases which reprove our cultural ancestors—including those of Greece, Rome, Italy and France —who had no notion of the extent to which their culture was going to be improved upon after the Oxford Conference on Church, Community and State in 1937. We know now that the highest achievements of the past, in art, in wisdom, in holiness, were but "stages in development" which we can teach our springalds to improve upon. We must not train them merely to receive the culture of the past, for that would be to regard the culture of the past as final. We must not impose culture upon the young, though we may impose upon them whatever political and social philosophy is in vogue. And yet the culture of Europe has deteriorated visibly within the memory of many who are by no means the oldest among us. And we know, that whether education can foster and improve culture or not, it can surely adulterate and degrade it. For there is no doubt that in our headlong rush to educate everybody, we are lowering our standards, and more and more abandoning the study of those subjects by which the essentials of our culture—of that part of it which is transmissible by education—are transmitted; destroying our ancient edifices to make ready the ground upon which the barbarian nomads of the future will encamp in their mechanised caravans.

The previous paragraph is to be considered only as an incidental flourish to relieve the feelings of the writer and perhaps of a few of his more sympathetic readers. It is no longer possible, as it might have been a hundred years ago, to find consolation in prophetic gloom; and such a means of escape would betray the intentions of this essay as stated in my introduction. If the reader goes so far as to agree that the kind of organisation of society which I have indicated is likely to be that most favourable to the growth and survival of a superior culture, he should then consider whether the *means* are themselves desirable as *ends:* for I have maintained that we cannot directly set about to create or improve culture—we can only will the means which are favourable to culture, and to do this we must be convinced that these means are themselves socially desirable. And beyond that point, we must proceed to consider how far these conditions of culture are possible, or even, in a particular situation at a particular time, compatible with all the immediate and pressing needs of an emergency. For one thing to avoid is a *universalised* planning; one thing to ascertain is the limits of the plannable. My enquiry, therefore, has been directed on the meaning of the word *culture:* so that everyone should at least pause to examine what this word means to him, and what it means to him in each particular context before using it. Even this modest aspiration might, if realised, have consequences in the policy and conduct of our "cultural" enterprises.

The Unity of European Culture

I

THIS is the first time that I have ever addressed a German-speaking audience, and before speaking on such a large subject, I think that I should present my credentials. For the unity of European culture is a very large subject indeed, and no one should try to speak about it, unless he has some particular knowledge or experience. Then he should start from that knowledge and experience and show what bearing it has on the general subject. I am a poet and a critic of poetry; I was also, from 1922 to 1939, the editor of a quarterly review. In this first talk I shall try to show what the first of these two professions has to do with my subject, and what conclusions my experience has led me to draw. So this is a series of talks about the unity of European culture from the point of view of a man of letters.

It has often been claimed that English, of all the languages of modern Europe, is the richest for the purposes of writing poetry. I think that this claim is justified. But please notice that when I say "richest for the purposes of writing poetry" I have been careful in my words: I do not mean that England has produced the greatest poets, or the greatest amount of great poetry. That is another question altogether. There are as great poets in other languages: Dante is certainly greater than Milton, and at least as great as Shakespeare. And even for the quantity of great poetry, I am not concerned to maintain that England has produced more. I simply say that the English language is the most remarkable medium for the poet to play with. It has the largest vocabulary: so large, that the command of it by any one poet seems meagre in comparison with its total wealth. But this is not the reason why it is the richest language for poetry: it is only a consequence of the real reason. This reason, in my opinion, is the variety of the elements of which English is made up. First, of course, there is the Germanic foundation, the element that you and we have in common. After this we find a considerable Scandinavian element, due in the first place to the Danish conquest. Then there is the Norman French element, after the Norman conquest. After this there followed a succession of French influences, traceable through words adopted at different periods. The sixteenth century saw a great increase of new words coined from the Latin; and the development of the language from the early sixteenth century to the middle of the seventeenth, was largely a process of testing new Latin words, assimilating some and rejecting others. And there is another element in English, not so easy to trace, but I think of considerable importance, the Celtic. But I am not thinking, in all this history, only of the Words, I am thinking, for poetry, primarily of the Rhythms. Each of these languages brought its own music: and the richness of the English language for poetry is first of all in its variety of metrical elements. There is the rhythm of early Saxon verse, the rhythm of the Norman French, the rhythm of the Welsh, and also the influence of generations of study of Latin and Greek poetry. And even today, the English language enjoys constant possibilities of refreshment from its several centres: apart from the vocabulary, poems by Englishmen, Welshmen, Scots and Irishmen, all written in English, continue to show differences in their Music.

The Unity of European Culture

I have not taken the trouble to talk to you in order to praise my own language; my reason for discussing it is that I think the reason why English is such a good language for poetry is that it is a composite from so many different European sources. As I have said, this does not imply that England must have produced the greatest poets. Art, as Goethe said, is in limitation: and a great poet is one who makes the most of the language that is given him. The truly great poet makes his language a great language. It is true, however, that we tend to think of each of the greater peoples as excelling in one art rather than another: Italy and then France in painting, Germany in music, and England in poetry. But, in the first place, no art has ever been the exclusive possession of any one country of Europe. And in the second place, there have been periods in which some other country than England has taken the lead in poetry. For instance, in the final years of the eighteenth century and the first quarter of the nineteenth, the Romantic movement in English poetry certainly dominated. But in the second half of the nineteenth century the greatest contribution to European poetry was certainly made in France. I refer to the tradition which starts with Baudelaire, and culminates in Paul Valéry. I venture to say that without this French tradition the work of three poets in other languages—and three very different from each other—I refer to W. B. Yeats, to Rainer Maria Rilke, and, if I may, to myself—would hardly be conceivable. And, so complicated are these literary influences, we must remember that this French movement itself owed a good deal to an American of Irish extraction: Edgar Allan Poe. And, even when one country and language leads all others, we must not assume that the poets to whom this is due are necessarily the greatest poets. I have spoken of the Romantic movement in England. But at that time Goethe was writing. I do not know of any standard by which one could gauge the relative greatness of Goethe and Wordsworth as poets, but the total work of Goethe has a scope which makes him a greater man. And no English poet contemporary with Wordsworth can enter into comparison with Goethe at all.

I have been leading up to another important truth about poetry in Europe. This is, that no one nation, no one language, would have achieved what it has, if the same art had not been cultivated in neighbouring countries and in different languages. We cannot understand any one European literature without knowing a good deal about the others. When we examine the history of poetry in Europe, we find a tissue of influences woven to and fro. There have been good poets who knew no language but their own, but even they have been subject to influences taken in and disseminated by other writers among their own people. Now, the possibility of each literature renewing itself, proceeding to new creative activity, making new discoveries in the use of words, depends on two things. First, its ability to receive and assimilate influences from abroad. Second, its ability to go back and learn from its own sources. As for the first, when the several countries of Europe are cut off from each other, when poets no longer read any literature but that in their own language, poetry in every country must deteriorate. As for the second, I wish to make this point especially: that every literature must have some sources which are peculiarly its own, deep in its own history; but, also, and at least equally important, are the sources which we share in common: that is, the literature of Rome, of Greece and of Israel.

There is a question which ought to be asked at this point, and which ought to be answered. What of the influences from outside Europe, of the great literature of Asia?

In the literature of Asia is great poetry. There is also profound wisdom and some very difficult metaphysics; but at the moment I am only concerned with poetry. I have no knowledge whatever of the Arabic, Persian, or Chinese languages. Long ago I studied the ancient Indian languages, and while I was chiefly interested at that time in Philosophy, I read a little poetry too; and I know that my own poetry shows the influence of Indian thought and sensibility. But generally, poets are not oriental scholars—I was never a scholar myself; and the influence of oriental literature upon poets is usually through translations. That there has been some influence of poetry of the East in the last century and a half is undeniable: to instance only English poetry, and in our own time, the poetical translations from the Chinese made by Ezra Pound, and those made by Arthur Waley, have probably been read by every poet writing in English. It is obvious that through individual interpreters, specially gifted for appreciating a remote culture, every literature may influence every other; and I emphasise this. For when I speak of the unity of European culture, I do not want to give the impression that I regard European culture as something cut off from every other. The frontiers of culture are not, and should not be, closed. But history makes a difference. Those countries which share the most history, are the most important to each other, with respect to their future literature. We have our common classics, of Greece and Rome; we have a common classic even in our several translations of the Bible.

What I have said of poetry is I think true of the other arts as well. The painter or the composer perhaps enjoys greater freedom, in that he is not limited by a particular language spoken only in one part of Europe: but in the practice of every art I think you find the same three elements: the local tradition, the common European tradition, and the influence of the art of one European country upon another. I only put this as a suggestion. I must limit myself to the art which I know most about. In poetry at least, no one country can be consistently highly creative for an indefinite period. Each country must have its secondary epochs, when no remarkable new development takes place: and so the centre of activity will shift to and fro between one country and another. And in poetry there is no such thing as complete originality, owing nothing to the past. Whenever a Virgil, a Dante, a Shakespeare, a Goethe is born, the whole future of European poetry is altered. When a great poet has lived, certain things have been done once for all, and cannot be achieved again; but, on the other hand, every great poet adds something to the complex material out of which future poetry will be written.

I have been speaking of the unity of European culture as illustrated by the arts and among the arts by the only one on which I am qualified to speak. I want to talk next time about the unity of European culture as illustrated by ideas. I mentioned at the beginning that during the period between the wars I had edited a quarterly review. My experience in this capacity, and my reflections upon it, will provide the starting point for my next talk.

II

I mentioned in my last talk that I had started and edited, between the wars, a literary review. I mentioned it first as one of my qualifications for speaking on this general subject. But also the history of this review illustrates some of the points that I want to make. So I hope that, after I have told you a little about it, you will begin to see its relevance to the subject of these talks.

We produced the first number of this review in the autumn of 1922, and decided to bring it to an end with the first number of the year 1939. So you see that its life covered nearly the same period that we call the years of peace. Except for a period of six months during which I tried the experiment of producing it monthly, its appearance was four times a year. In starting this review, I had the aim of bringing together the best in new thinking and new writing in its time, from all the countries of Europe that had anything to contribute to the common good. Of course it was designed primarily for English readers, and therefore all foreign contributions had to appear in an English translation. There may be a function for reviews published in two or more languages, and in two or more countries simultaneously. But even such reviews, searching all Europe for contributions, must contain some pieces of translation, if they are to be read by everybody. And they cannot take the place of those periodicals which appear in each country and which are intended primarily for the readers in that country. So my review was an ordinary English periodical, only of international scope. I sought, therefore, first to find out who were the best writers, unknown or little known outside of their own country, whose work deserved to be known more widely. Second, I tried to establish relations with those literary periodicals abroad, the aims of which corresponded most nearly to my own. I mention, as instances, the *Nouvelle Revue Française* (then edited by Jacques Rivière, and subsequently by Jean Paulhan), the *Neue Rundschau*, the *Neue Schweizer Rundschau*, the *Revista de Occidente* in Spain, *Il Convegno* and others in Italy. These connexions developed very satisfactorily, and it was no fault of any of the editors concerned, if they subsequently languished. I am still of the opinion, twenty-three years after I began, and seven years after I ended, that the existence of such a network of independent reviews, at least one in every capital of Europe, is necessary for the transmission of ideas— and to make possible the circulation of ideas while they are still fresh. The editors of such reviews, and if possible the more regular contributors, should be able to get to know each other personally, to visit each other, to entertain each other, and to exchange ideas in conversation. In any one such periodical, of course, there must be much that will be of interest only to readers of its own nation and language. But their co-operation should continually stimulate that circulation of influence of thought and sensibility, between nation and nation in Europe, which fertilises and renovates from abroad the literature of each one of them. And through such co-operation, and the friendships between men of letters which ensue from it, should emerge into public view those works of literature which are not only of local, but of European significance.

The particular point, however, of my talking about my aims, in relation to a review which has been dead for seven years, is that in the end they failed. And I attribute this failure chiefly to the gradual closing of the mental frontiers of Europe. A kind of cultural autarchy followed inevitably upon political and economic autarchy. This did not merely interrupt communications: I believe that it had a numbing effect upon creative activity within every country. The blight fell first upon our friends in Italy. And after 1933 contributions from Germany became more and more difficult to find. Some of our friends died; some disappeared; some merely became silent. Some went abroad, cut off from their own cultural roots. One of the latest found and the last lost, was that great critic and good European, who died a few months ago: Theodor Haecker. And, from much of the German writing that I saw in the 30's, by authors previously unknown to me, I formed the opinion that the newer German writers had less and less to say to Europe; that they were more and more saying what could be understood, if understood at all, only in Germany. What happened in Spain is more confused; the tumult of the civil war was hardly favourable to thought and creative writing; and that war divided and scattered, even when it did not destroy, many of her ablest writers. In France there was still free intellectual activity, but more and more harassed and limited by political anxieties and forebodings, and by the internal divisions which political prepossessions set up. England, though manifesting some symptoms of the same malady, remained apparently intact. But I think that our literature of that period suffered by being more and more restricted to its own resources, as well as by the obsession with politics.

The Unity of European Culture

Now the first comment I have to make on this story of a literary review which had clearly failed of its purpose several years before events brought it to an end, is this. A universal concern with politics does not unite, it divides. It unites those politically minded folk who agree, across the frontiers of nations, against some other international group who hold opposed views. But it tends to destroy the cultural unity of Europe. *The Criterion,* for that is the name of the review which I edited, had, I believe, a definite character and cohesion, although its contributors were men holding the most diverse political, social and religious views. I think also that it had a definite congeniality with the foreign periodicals with which it associated itself. The question of a writer's political, social or religious views simply did not enter into our calculations, or into those of our foreign colleagues. What the common basis was, both at home and abroad, is not easy to define. In those days it was unnecessary to formulate it; at the present time it becomes impossible to formulate. I should say that it was a common concern for the highest standards both of thought and of expression, that it was a common curiosity and openness of mind to new ideas. The ideas with which you did not agree, the opinions which you could not accept, were as important to you as those which you found immediately acceptable. You examined them without hostility, and with the assurance that you could learn from them. In other words, we could take for granted an interest, a delight, in ideas for their own sake, in the free play of intellect. And I think that also, among our chief contributors and colleagues, there was something which was not so much a consciously held belief, but an unconscious assumption. Something which had never been doubted, and therefore had no need to rise to the conscious level of affirmation. It was the assumption that there existed an international fraternity of men of letters, within Europe: a bond which did not replace, but was perfectly compatible with, national loyalties, religious loyalties, and differences of political philosophy. And that it was our business not so much to make any particular ideas prevail, as to maintain intellectual activity on the highest level.

I do not think that *The Criterion,* in its final years, wholly succeeded in living up to this ideal. I think that in the later years it tended to reflect a particular point of view, rather than to illustrate a variety of views on that plane. But I do not think that this was altogether the fault of the editor: I think that it came about partly from the pressure of circumstances of which I have spoken.

I am not pretending that politics and culture have nothing to do with each other. If they could be kept completely apart, the problem might be simpler than it is. A nation's political structure affects its culture, and in turn is affected by that culture. But nowadays we take too much interest in each other's domestic politics, and at the same time have very little contact with each other's culture. The confusion of culture and politics may lead in two different directions. It may make a nation intolerant of every culture but its own, so that it feels impelled to stamp out, or to remould, every culture surrounding it. An error of the Germany of Hitler was to assume that every other culture than that of Germany was either decadent or barbaric. Let us have an end of such assumptions. The other direction in which the confusion of culture and politics may lead, is towards the ideal of a world state in which there will, in the end, be only one uniform world culture. I am not here criticising any schemes for world organisation. Such schemes belong to the plane of engineering, of devising machinery. Machinery is necessary, and the more perfect the machine the better. But culture is something that must grow; you cannot build a tree, you can only plant it, and care for it, and wait for it to mature in its due time; and when it is grown you must not complain if you find that from an acorn has come an oak, and not an elm-tree. And a political structure is partly construction, and partly growth; partly machinery, and the same machinery, if good, is equally good for all peoples; and partly growing with and from the nation's culture, and in that respect different from that of other nations. For the health of the culture of Europe two conditions are required: that the culture of each country should be unique, and that the different cultures should recognise their relationship to each other, so that each should be susceptible of influence from the others. And this is possible because there is a common element in European culture, an interrelated history of thought and feeling and behaviour, an interchange of arts and of ideas.

In my last talk I shall try to define this common element more closely: and I think that will require my saying a little more about the meaning that I give to this word "Culture," which I have been using so constantly.

III

I said at the end of my second talk that I should want to make a little clearer what I mean when I use the term culture. Like "democracy," this is a term which needs to be, not only defined, but illustrated, almost every time we use it. And it is necessary to be clear about what we mean by "culture," so that we may be clear about the distinction between the material organisation of Europe, and the spiritual organism of Europe. If the latter dies, then what you organise will not be Europe, but merely a mass of human beings speaking several different languages. And there will be no longer any justification for their continuing to speak different languages, for they will no longer have anything to say which cannot be said equally well in any language: they will, in short, have no longer anything to say in poetry. I have already affirmed that there can be no "European" culture if the several countries are isolated from each other: I add now that there can be no European culture if these countries are reduced to identity. We need variety in unity: not the unity of organisation, but the unity of nature.

By "culture," then, I mean first of all what the anthropologists mean: the way of life of a particular people living together in one place. That culture is made visible in their arts, in their social system, in their habits and customs, in their religion. But these things added together do not constitute the culture, though we often speak for convenience as if they did. These things are simply the parts into which a culture can be anatomised, as a human body can. But just as a man is something more than an assemblage of the various constituent parts of his body, so a culture is more than the assemblage of its arts, customs, and religious beliefs. These things all act upon each other, and fully to understand one you have to understand all. Now there are of course higher cultures and lower cultures, and the higher cultures in general are distinguished by differentiation of function, so that you can speak of the less cultured and the more cultured strata of society, and finally, you can speak of individuals as being exceptionally cultured. The culture of an artist or a philosopher is distinct from that of a mine worker or field labourer; the culture of a poet will be somewhat different from that of a politician; but in a healthy society these are all parts of the same culture; and the artist, the poet, the philosopher, the politician and the labourer will have a culture in common, which they do not share with other people of the same occupations in other countries.

Now it is obvious that one unity of culture is that of the people who live together and speak the same language: because speaking the same language means thinking, and feeling, and having emotions, rather differently from people who use a different language. But the cultures of different peoples do affect each other: in the world of the future it looks as if every part of the world would affect every other part. I have suggested earlier, that the cultures of the different countries of Europe have in the past derived very great benefit from their influence upon each other. I have suggested that the national culture which isolates itself voluntarily, or the national culture which is cut off from others by circumstances which it cannot control, suffers from this isolation. Also, that the country which receives culture from abroad, without having anything to give in return, and the country which aims to impose its culture on another, without accepting anything in return, will both suffer from this lack of reciprocity.

There is something more than a general exchange of culture influences, however. You cannot even attempt to trade equally with every other nation: there will be some who need the kind of goods that you produce, more than others do, and there will be some who produce the goods you need yourselves, and others who do not. So cultures of people speaking different languages can be more or less closely related: and sometimes so closely related that we can speak of their having a common culture. Now when we speak of "European culture," we mean the identities which we can discover in the various national cultures; and of course even within Europe, some cultures are more closely related than others. Also, one culture within a group of cultures can be closely related, on different sides, to two cultures which are not closely related to each other. Your cousins are not all cousins of each other, for some are on the father's side and some on the mother's. Now, just as I have refused to consider the culture of Europe simply as the sum of a number of unrelated cultures in the same area, so I refused to separate the world into quite unrelated cultural groups; I refused to draw any absolute line between East and West, between Europe and Asia. There are, however, certain common features in Europe, which make it possible to speak of a European culture. What are they?

125

The Unity of European Culture

The dominant force in creating a common culture between peoples each of which has its distinct culture, is religion. Please do not, at this point, make a mistake in anticipating my meaning. This is not a religious talk, and I am not setting out to convert anybody. I am simply stating a fact. I am not so much concerned with the communion of Christian believers today; I am talking about the common tradition of Christianity which has made Europe what it is, and about the common cultural elements which this common Christianity has brought with it. If Asia were converted to Christianity tomorrow, it would not thereby become a part of Europe. It is in Christianity that our arts have developed; it is in Christianity that the laws of Europe have —until recently—been rooted. It is against a background of Christianity that all our thought has significance. An individual European may not believe that the Christian Faith is true, and yet what he says, and makes, and does, will all spring out of his heritage of Christian culture and depend upon that culture for its meaning. Only a Christian culture could have produced a Voltaire or a Nietzsche. I do not believe that the culture of Europe could survive the complete disappearance of the Christian Faith. And I am convinced of that, not merely because I am a Christian myself, but as a student of social biology. If Christianity goes, the whole of our culture goes. Then you must start painfully again, and you cannot put on a new culture ready made. You must wait for the grass to grow to feed the sheep to give the wool out of which your new coat will be made. You must pass through many centuries of barbarism. We should not live to see the new culture, nor would our great-great-great-grandchildren: and if we did, not one of us would be happy in it.

To our Christian heritage we owe many things besides religious faith. Through it we trace the evolution of our arts, through it we have our conception of Roman Law which has done so much to shape the Western World, through it we have our conceptions of private and public morality. And through it we have our common standards of literature, in the literatures of Greece and Rome. The Western World has its unity in this heritage, in Christianity and in the ancient civilisations of Greece, Rome and Israel, from which, owing to two thousand years of Christianity, we trace our descent. I shall not elaborate this point. What I wish to say is, that this unity in the common elements of culture, throughout many centuries, is the true bond between us. No political and economic organisation, however much goodwill it commands, can supply what this culture unity gives. If we dissipate or throw away our common patrimony of culture, then all the organisation and planning of the most ingenious minds will not help us, or bring us closer together.

The unity of culture, in contrast to the unity of political organisation, does not require us all to have only one loyalty: it means that there will be a variety of loyalties. It is wrong that the only duty of the individual should be held to be towards the State; it is fantastic to hold that the supreme duty of every individual should be towards a Super-State. I will give one instance of what I mean by a variety of loyalties. No university ought to be merely a national institution, even if it is supported by the nation. The universities of Europe should have their common ideals, they should have their obligations towards each other. They should be independent of the governments of the countries in which they are situated. They should not be institutions for the training of an efficient bureaucracy, or for equipping scientists to get the better of foreign scientists; they should stand for the preservation of learning, for the pursuit of truth, and in so far as men are capable of it, the attainment of wisdom.

There is much more that I should have liked to say in this last talk, but I must now be very brief. My last appeal is to the men of letters of Europe, who have a special responsibility for the preservation and transmission of our common culture. We may hold very different political views: our common responsibility is to preserve our common culture uncontaminated by political influences. It is not a question of sentiment: it does not matter so much whether we like each other, or praise each other's writings. What matters is that we should recognise our relationship and mutual dependence upon each other. What matters is our inability, without each other, to produce those excellent works which mark a superior civilisation. We cannot, at present, hold much communication with each other. We cannot visit each other as private individuals; if we travel at all, it can only be through government agencies and with official duties. But we can at least try to save something of those goods of which we are the common trustees: the legacy of Greece, Rome and Israel, and the legacy of Europe throughout the last 2,000 years. In a world which has seen such material devastation as ours, these spiritual possessions are also in imminent peril.